# The Way We Write

## Interviews with Award-winning Writers

edited by Barbara Baker

continuum

**Continuum**

The Tower Building
11 York Road
London
SE1 7NX

80 Maiden Lane
Suite 704
New York
NY 10038

First published 2006
Reprinted 2006
Paperback edition 2007

**British Library Cataloguing-in-Publication Data**
A catalogue record for this book is available from the British Library.

ISBN-10:  0-8264-9122-7 (hardback)
          0-8264-9505-2 (paperback)
ISBN-13:  9780826491220 (hardback)
          9780826495051 (paperback)

**Library of Congress Cataloging-in-Publication Data**
A catalog record for this book is available from the Library of Congress.

Typeset by Servis Filmsetting Ltd, Manchester
Printed and bound in Great Britain by
MPG Books Ltd, Bodmin, Cornwall

For two good friends to whom I owe much
Jeremy Over
and
Madeleine Marie Slavick

# Contents

# Contents by genre

# Acknowledgements

My biggest thanks go to my husband Robin, who is always the first reader of my work, and whose critical opinions and help are invaluable. My gratitude extends to many people who have generously given advice and support: Kavita Jindal, Gaynor Lloyd, Rebecca Lloyd, Alexandra Lynch, Jeremy Over, Madeleine Marie Slavick, Marjorie Sweetko and, particularly, Jacqueline Young. I would like to thank the organizers of 'Words by the Water' Cumbrian Literature Festival, and the staff of Continuum International Publishing Group Ltd, especially Anna Sandeman.

I acknowledge all publishers from whose books passages are quoted: Bloodaxe Books Ltd, Dalkey Archive Press, Faber & Faber Ltd, UK and Graywolf Press, US (for the extract from 'The Landing' in *Landing Light* by Don Paterson, 2003), Grove Atlantic Ltd, HarperCollins Publishers Ltd, Macmillan Publishers Ltd, The Maia Press Ltd, Methuen Publishing Ltd (for the extract from *Educating Rita* by Willy Russell, 1985), Penguin Books (UK), Peterloo Poets (for 'Ask A Silly Question' in *Consequences* by U. A. Fanthorpe, 2000), The Random House Group Ltd, Scholastic Ltd, Theatre Communications Group Inc for the extract from *In the Heart of America* © 1994, 1997, 2001 Naomi Wallace in *In the Heart of America and Other Plays* © 2001, and finally The Waywiser Press.

# Introduction

Samuel Johnson wrote, 'What is written without effort is read without pleasure.'

This book reveals what that effort, or craft, entails. Both the mental and physical aspects of the creative process are discussed by 18 eminent, contrasting writers. Children's writers, playwrights/screenplay writers, novelists/short-story writers and poets were interviewed: they are as diverse as they are illuminating.

Writers' methods are demystified as they divulge why they write, who they write for, where and how often they write, recurring themes in their work, their problems and achievements. As well as describing technique, these writers talk openly about the more elusive sides of their work, such as inspiration or to what extent their writing is autobiographical. Their interviews are intimate, honest, informative and at times humorous. The reader not only learns about writing, but also gains a unique insight into each writer's personality.

T. S. Eliot wrote, 'Most editors are failed writers – but so are most writers.' All these writers are winners. They have all been awarded prizes, and their work demonstrates sustained literary merit, rather than flash-in-the pan popularity. As an example of their style, some lines from a work by each writer are quoted at the start of every interview. These passages were chosen by the writers themselves.

There is no set formula for successful creative writing, but examining what the interviewees share in common, and how they differ, is revealing. First, the shared traits. Most of these writers, with the surprising exception of Julia Donaldson, got published with unusual ease. Only two of them (Tracy Chevalier and Naomi Wallace) had any formal training. Many found poetry a very useful way into writing. As novelist Harry Mathews expresses it, 'I think poetry is the best possible training for a prose writer.' All of the writers stressed the centrality of language, and the importance of craft (or graft!). Struggle was a word that was used a lot, as was the phrase 'it makes it all worthwhile', implying that suffering is first involved. Writers commonly experience feelings of frustration, expressed by William Faulkner when he wrote, 'The work never matches the dream of perfection the artist has to start with.'

Another quotation which seems to be apt for creative writing in each genre is from the American author, poet and philosopher David Thoreau, who wrote, 'Not that the story need be long, but it will take a long while to make it short.' Most writers interviewed talk of the effort as well as enjoyment involved in making every word count, cutting whatever is superfluous; and generally, the huge amount of revision that is usually involved. As one of them, poet Al Alvarez puts it, 'I am not a very good writer, but I am a marvellous rewriter', and elsewhere, 'Writing is a craft as well as an art.' In her book *The Faith of a Writer*, novelist Joyce Carol Oates reiterates and expounds this view when she writes, 'Without craft, art remains private. Without art, craft is merely hackwork', while in her interview she says, 'rewriting/revising/reimagining is the very life's blood of the creative enterprise'.

For the majority, but perhaps particularly for Don Paterson, 'The whole point is the process.' Paterson does not even like being called a poet, since, 'poetry describes an act, not necessarily a permanent disposition'. And again, there were several similarities in how that act, whether it was writing fiction, poetry, or plays, was achieved. Both Paterson and novelist Harry Mathews deliberately challenge themselves, almost, it would seem, making the process as hard as possible, and both are also acutely aware of the artificial aspect of the written word. As Mathews says, 'reading is a linguistic experience', rather than any kind of substitute for life.

The contributors to this book tend to write for themselves, not an imagined audience: the end product has to satisfy their own critical criteria. Even at this level of success, they each have to overcome the dread of the blank page, and a fear of failure. Virtually all the writers do not have the whole plot of a novel, play, or children's story worked out in advance. And on the whole they do not have strict schedules, nor work a prescribed number of hours each day. Michael Bond came up with a useful tip in this regard, stating, 'I like leaving off when I could go on, because then I can start the next day.'

Many interviewees claimed that writing, for them, was a kind of addiction, almost a drug, which has the ability to temporarily blot out all other aspects of life. When it goes well, writers get an incredible high, a knowledge that something has worked, a discovery of something they didn't know before, or didn't realize they knew. As novelist Graham Swift puts it, 'writing is a leap into the unknown that you take with the sort of rope of the imagination to hang on to'. There was a common fear and wonder while writing, which ideally should be mirrored in the reader.

But perhaps ironically, what most good writers are ultimately aiming for is something that reads beautifully, without the style (or craft) being noticeable, yet where the principles of structure, tone and language are as important as the content. Writers are also hoping to give the reader a memorable experience, one expressed by Alan Bennett in his play *The History Boys*, in some lines given to the teacher Hector: 'The best moments in reading are when you come across something – a thought, a feeling, a way of looking at things – which you had thought special or particular to you. Now here it is, set down by someone else, a person you have never met, someone even who is long since dead. And it is as if a hand has come out and taken yours.' At their best, all the interviewed writers achieve this.

These then, are some of the things the contributors to this book have in common: now for the differences. A little fewer than half the interviewees started writing after the age of 20; more than half write by hand rather than with a computer – and these include, unexpectedly, four of the novelists. And while one might think that the starting point for most writers is the same, in fact it is not. Playwright Willy Russell and children's writer Michael Morpurgo find a voice first, and from that everything else develops. For novelist Tracy Chevalier it is generally an image that is the inspiration. An idea, theme, or subject spark the work of playwright Naomi Wallace, poet Benjamin Zephaniah, and novelists Margaret Drabble and Sara Maitland. Similarly, children's writer Raymond Briggs says, 'I get bugged by an idea. It is like a niggle, and you do it [write] to get rid of this irritant.' For children's writer Michael Bond, it is the character that drives his stories, and in fact, takes over. Fellow children's writer, Eleanor Updale, says she is story-driven, though she confesses, 'I really know the characters so well – almost laying the table for them!'

The length of time taken to write also varies tremendously, perhaps the most extreme example being U. A. Fanthorpe: 'One poem I wrote took four years, but another I wrote overnight.' Many writers like to work in a room of their own, for others, like Don Paterson, a noisy café is most conducive. Among the novelists, some only write in the first person, some have linear plots, some combine the real with the unreal. There are also differences in attitude and confidence. Naomi Wallace (playwright) showed poems to her teachers at school to make them like her; Eleanor Updale (children's writer) submitted her own poems to the school magazine under the name of her best friend, considering writing the province of others. Tracy Chevalier writes in the secure knowledge that her book will be read by the public; fellow novelist Margaret Drabble worries that what she is writing will be turned down by the publishers. It is fascinating that in examining the ways the contributors write, they also disclose much about themselves.

In summary, all the writers have tremendous commitment to their craft, but solutions to the problems of creative writing are various, and are dependent upon the individual's personality. As a result this book is suggestive rather than prescriptive, inspirational rather than didactic. It does not aspire to comprehensiveness, nor does it offer single solutions – though some of the methodologies and aesthetic strategies described could usefully be adopted by others. It is important for each individual writer to find a method and routine with which they are comfortable, while also challenging themselves and being experimental. Writing is idiosyncratic, as is this book.

So, for my own part, I shall briefly describe my methods in compiling the book. Having read each author's work, and drawn up a list of questions, I either interviewed the writer in person, or over the phone. In both cases I taped the conversation. Next I transcribed the taped interview, omitting my questions, onto my computer. I then printed it out and made pencil alterations. If there was repetition I left it out, and in order to make the interviews flow, I frequently altered the order of paragraphs, but not the writer's words. I then transferred these changes to the computer. I would repeat this process once or twice more, until I was satisfied.

Choosing the interviewees could be nothing but subjective. My criteria were to include writers whose work I admired, who were best-known in one genre. I also aimed to select writers whose style was very varied, and who were able to discuss their methods eloquently. I was not disappointed, and I hope readers will not be either. Each interview has its own distinct character, tone and register. I was interested to find that of all the children's writers I approached, virtually all agreed to be interviewed. The playwrights was the most difficult group from whom to gain acceptance, and I think this has something to do with the fact that they generally do fewer readings and signings and discussion of their work.

The letters declining the request for interview were interesting too: I shall just quote three examples. To my surprise,

Michael Frayn wrote: 'Thanks for your letter. It's very nice of you to suggest interviewing me about the way I write. I've thought about it, though, and discover that I can think of nothing whatsoever to say about it. I'm sorry to be so dull.' Perhaps less surprising was the card from Alan Bennett: 'Thank you for your letter and for all the good things you say. The reason why I don't do interviews is I don't talk very well and also I find the more I talk the less I write. And if I don't write nobody will want to hear me talk anyway. Thank you for asking me, though. I appreciate it.'

Finally, Kazuo Ishiguro expressed what I think a lot of writers feel when he wrote: 'Unfortunately I'm under enormous pressure of work at the moment, and moreover, on reflection, I feel I'd rather not talk too much about my actual working methods. I know many authors like to do so, but I don't feel easy about it myself, for a number of different reasons. So I hope you'll forgive me if I duck out of this one. I'm sorry about this. Nevertheless, I wish you the best with your book and look forward to seeing it in the shops.'

These polite refusals make me especially grateful to all the writers who agreed to contribute. They are all busy and their time is precious. Moreover I think there is a generally held feeling that there is a certain alchemy involved with writing and that in discussing it, the magic might go. So to each of the extremely generous writers whom I interviewed, I owe an enormous debt of thanks. I also apologize to the few who, owing to confines of space, unfortunately had to be left out. This book has been a pleasure and a privilege to write. I hope it will inspire and help other writers, and engross all readers, encouraging them to read more.

# Al Alvarez

*Al Alvarez is a poet, writer and critic: he is always described thus, even though his books of non-fiction outnumber those of poems.*

*Born in London in 1929 into a Jewish family, he was sent away to public school and then went to Oxford. Perhaps because he was passionate about D. H. Lawrence, he married the daughter of Lawrence's wife in 1956. He was divorced five years later, and married his present wife, Anne (the subject of the poem below), in 1966. As poetry editor of the* Observer, *Al Alvarez has known most of the leading poets of the second half of the last century, and introduced British readers to the work of many of them. He was friends with both Ted Hughes and Sylvia Plath, and was one of the last people to see Plath alive. He published many of her last poems, which she would read to him in his studio, trusting his judgement. Alvarez was an influential critic: his anthology* The New Poetry *(1962) scandalized the literary community of the time by championing American style rather than British gentility.*

*Meanwhile Alvarez also went rock climbing (perhaps difficult to imagine in someone who now walks with a stick) and played poker, writing books on these pastimes, which are now regarded as classics. He also wrote novels ('I am not really a novelist, and have written three novels to prove it') and poems. He is not a prolific poet: his latest book was published almost 25 years after its predecessor. But his lyric accomplishment and direct emotional impact were worth waiting for. While his early poems were mainly concerned with the loss of love, separation and death, the new ones are largely preoccupied with love, dreaming, wonderment and gratitude.*

*I first read Alvarez's work when I came across* The Savage God *in a public library soon after it was published. This powerful study of suicide, and of Sylvia Plath in particular, led me to read Plath's novel* The Bell

Jar *(1963), then her poetry, and later, the poetry of Al Alvarez. I have much to thank him for.*

## Selected Bibliography

Poetry
*Autumn to Autumn and Selected Poems 1953–1976* (1978), *New and Selected Poems* (2002)

Novels
*Hers* (1974), *Day of Atonement* (1991)

Non-fiction
*The Savage God: A Study in Suicide* (1971), *Life After Marriage: Scenes from Divorce* (1982), *Offshore: A North Sea Journey* (1986), *Poker: Bets, Bluffs and Bad Beats* (2000)

Criticism
*Samuel Beckett* (1973), *The Writer's Voice* (2005)

Autobiography
*Where Did It All Go Right?* (1999)

This poem is from *New and Selected Poems*:

Anne Dancing

You sashay in, twenty years-old again,
Sweatshirt and jeans, eyes closed, a cat-like smile,
Self-satisfied, self-absorbed, hips swaying,
Weaving your intricate steps across
The intricate carpet. The merest glance

At me does it. You're a North American
College girl out on a date, a '50s-style
Dazzler – great legs, cute ass, sweet smile.
    That's Satchmo playing
Your youth back loud and clear. You toss
Your greying, lovely head. You say, 'Come on, let's dance.'

\*     \*     \*

What I always say is that I write prose for a living and poetry
when I get lucky. I have never wanted to have to rely on poetry:
you can only write a poem when you have got your head in the
right place. You have to be kind of open – it is like the ground
outside can't receive the rain if it is frozen solid. When I was
younger I wrote more, as you do. I am a lyric poet, I don't write
long poems, and they are mostly love poems or 'unlove' poems.
I think, as I have got older, my prose has got a lot better and the
gap has slightly closed, in that the poems I have written in the
last ten years or so are easier in themselves. The early ones are
deeply depressed.

    I chose 'Anne Dancing' to quote, apart from the fact that it is
short, because it is a love poem to my wife. Also, it has a trick in
it, which is not immediately obvious. I am always very concerned
with, not the inner music, because that has awful pompous over-
tones, but the inner movement of a line, or getting the lines to
come alive. Here there are two stanzas, and the lines in the
stanzas don't rhyme, but they rhyme across the stanzas. So the
first line of the first stanza rhymes with the first line of the second
stanza, and so on, which is a way of holding the poem together
without making it sound formal.

    I find strict rhyming schemes rather too constricting, but it is
easier to write a sonnet than free verse that works. Free verse
which is just cut up chunks of prose is easy, but that is just a poem
that failed. A real poem is integral, and intricate, and musical,

but not in a 'plonkity plonk' way. I am a frustrated musician. My family were all seriously musical, and I was brought up in a house where all you could hear was classical music all the time. I do that myself now. I have Radio 3 on all the time, and I have a lot of musical friends, like the pianist Alfred Brendel. When I was a very little kid I kept saying, 'I want to learn the piano.' Any normal parent would have done something about it, but mine never got round to it!

In my dreams now, I would have preferred to be, say, a pianist, or a composer. But that is a bit like Peter Cook, when he said, 'I could have been a judge if I had had the Latin.' But I feel the inner music, or movement of language, is hugely important. Inner rhythm is the one thing you can't fake. You can *hear* when a poet is writing about something from the way the line moves. I am not talking about regular metre, where you know where every thump or stress is going to come, but the movement that is very unpredictable, like, 'Busily seeking with a continual change' which is by Thomas Wyatt, and you think, 'Wow! He was really being shaken by something.' That is what I am on the listen for, and I try to write poems that are alive in that way. There is quite an early poem of mine called 'The Gate' where I actually heard it, before I got the words: I had some kind of rhythm in my head.

The interesting thing is that the really good poems come very fast, and then you tinker with them. I think one of the best poems I ever wrote is called 'He Said, She Said', which is about 30 lines long, and I wrote it in about 20 minutes and then fiddled with it a bit. The good ones are like finding something, or being given a present. I do worry over every word, but if the poem is good to start with, I do not find that that is a long process.

The difference between writing prose and poetry is that I am an obsessional rewriter of prose. Then you see the thing printed and you still see some awful blunder where you repeated a word just over the page or something. But if you have a real ear as a poet, you can't do that. A poem is like one of those giant locks they have in bank vaults, with dozens of tumblers, which all have to fall into place. And when they fall into place, you open the door with a click, the poem is finished, goodbye; it goes out to the world and has nothing more to do with you. But until every tumbler is in place, it is not finished, and if you have got any kind of aesthetic consciousness, you know this.

I think it is harder for me, because I am also a critic. From about 1956 to 1966, I was poetry editor and reviewer for the *Observer*, which was then a very serious place for poetry to be published – *the* place. Can you imagine that now? Half a page of poems by unknowns on a Sunday! But I felt one shouldn't wear two hats in a job, so although I published my own poetry in America at the time, I didn't publish much of my own in England. I also did an anthology called *The New Poetry*. I was a poet, I was one of them, but I felt that I shouldn't put my own poems in, which I now see was a peculiar career move.

*The New Poetry* was supposed to be what was happening in the poetry scene in the mid-50s. But basically, I didn't much like what was happening in English poetry then. I thought it was a very restricted movement, but it was part of the deal with Penguin that the book had to represent what was happening. So I wrote a rather fighting introduction. I was much more impressed and moved by what Americans like Robert Lowell and John Berryman were beginning to do: using private lives, but still within the intellectual high-minded tradition of Eliot and modernism. But they were using very private material and making marvellous poems out of it. So in my introduction, 'Beyond the Gentility Principal', I wrote that this was the thing to do, and this was not what was happening in English poetry.

I *know* that this meant a huge amount to Sylvia Plath, because she talked about it. *The New Poetry* came out in the spring of 1962, just when Sylvia really started to hit her stride: the wonderful great year before she died. She would come round and read her poems to me, and I read my poems to her. The one she liked best was a poem called 'Lost'. We used to talk as two poets trying to do the same thing. We were on the same wavelength, whereas I was clearly not on the same wavelength as people like Philip Larkin and Kingsley Amis, but I was, with poets like the young Thom Gunn, and Ted Hughes, and Sylvia.

I happened to be the one who was making a critical case for their kind of writing, saying that this was what mattered, rather than the movement poets, who were like essayists making a point with a middle, beginning and end. It was a very exciting time. Lowell and Berryman had hardly appeared in print in England until they were in the *Observer*. It was the same with the Czech poet Miroslav Holub, and the Polish poet Zbigniew Herbert, who was probably the greatest poet of the second half of the twentieth century. And I was quite literally the only poetry editor who would publish those late poems of Sylvia's.

The last time I saw Sylvia was on Christmas Eve, 1962. In January 1963, in the days when I still went to literary parties, a subsequently very renowned literary editor asked, 'Have you seen Sylvia recently?' and I replied, 'No, not for a couple of weeks, why?' and he said, 'I think she is in a pretty terrible state.' I asked, 'How do you know?' and he said, 'Well, she sent me some poems.' So I said, 'Oh! Which ones?' because she had read me most of her work. He said, ' "Daddy", "Lady Lazarus". . .': about 20 poems, now all anthology pieces. I said, 'Fantastic! Which ones are you going to print?' And he replied, 'None; they were too extreme for my taste. I sent them back.' Nobody recognized her talent. *The Savage God* was the first time anyone wrote about Sylvia.

But I was unable to alleviate Sylvia's terrible loneliness and despair. She needed someone to take care of her and it was not a role I could fill. I had a very bad first marriage, and then a kind of wild period. In the middle of that period, which was actually two or three months before Sylvia died, Anne and I got together. I was a kind of real crazy guy in those days, and didn't want to get caught by anybody, and Anne was very chary of getting caught up also. So we kept on coming together and then breaking apart: on and off like the lights of Piccadilly Circus. It was obviously right, but somehow something kept getting in the way.

Finally Anne moved in with a guy, and I had several girlfriends, but one I was really involved with and thought I was in love with (like you do, because she was giving me a hard time). I hadn't seen Anne for months and I had a dream about her. I dreamt that she and I were dancing, which is something we did very well together. And I pushed her out at arm's length and looked at her, and I realized that her hair was white, and that mine was white, and that we were together and totally happy. And 25 years later I wrote the poem.

Oddly enough, at the time of the dream, we got back together and then broke up again, and finally it was getting more and more ridiculous that we weren't together. Then I heard a terribly funny joke. I was with my son from my first marriage, and I happened to be driving past Anne's door, and I hadn't seen her for about three months, but she was coming down the steps, with the rubbish to put out. She was looking terribly depressed, and I slammed the breaks on and dashed up the steps and said I'd just heard this wonderfully funny joke and I told it to her, and it got her laughing. What I didn't know was that she was training in analysis, and the analyst had gone mad, and she was in a kind of suicidal depression, and it was the first time she had laughed for months. If you can make each other laugh, everything works.

I tell that story in my biography, *Where Did It All Go Right?* which is probably the book I am most pleased with. I am a very, very, very slow writer of prose, which is a terrible disadvantage since I am a professional writer. I am not a very good writer, but I am a marvellous rewriter! It kind of kills me to get the stuff down on the page. I wrote my latest small book, *The Writer's Voice*, ten times before I got the tone right. Writing for me is a struggle.

Every time I sit down in front of a piece of paper, or the computer screen, I go through the same process. I do not know how to write a sentence, forget a paragraph! And then even if I did know how to write a sentence, I haven't got anything to say. And anyway I don't want to say anything. Those are my feelings at the start of writing prose. Poems are different. If you can just shut up and open up, they come as a gift. And then I feel that I have got something as perfect as I am able to do it at that moment. You may look back at it later, and think, 'Actually, that poem is pretty awful.' The reason why my collected works is so small, and seems to get smaller every time I do a new selection, is that I throw a lot of poems away. I am very self-critical.

Writing is a craft as well as an art, and you want to make it as good as you possibly can; like making a table. Nowadays that is not always the case with writers. It is easier to parade your personality than to write something that really works and is beautiful: I don't mean it has to be chiselled in a Theophile Gautier way, I mean like some of the little Yeats lyrics which are perfection – nothing can be moved. But I think what is terrific about poems is that you are making something as perfect as you can. And however obsessional and perfectionist you are, you can never quite do it with prose.

I write longhand and then, when I have something there, I put it on a computer. When it is longhand, it is attached to you, but when it is on the computer you can see it at a distance. I write at the top of the house – a bit like a squirrel in his nest. I have a study, and spend a lot of time looking at the computer screen or at the view. Being a writer is very unromantic. My wife is a child psychoanalyst, and like hers, writing is a sedentary, middle-class occupation, but she at least gets to see patients. I don't see anybody! One of the blessings of playing poker was that it used to get me out of my study and into a card room in a casino to play.

Readings get you out, and I quite like them, although I only do one about every five years, but I hate performance poetry. And

I don't really exist as a poet. Now, at 75, the comments are 'Oh! He's still alive.' The poetry world is extremely cliquey. My latest book of poems wasn't reviewed in the *Observer*, for instance, or the *Times Literary Supplement*, because I am not part of that gang. The world is full of weird ironies. I have written two books about poker, and poker is suddenly hot.

*The Biggest Game in Town*, which I wrote about 20 years ago, was read by all poker players, but no one bought it. Now there is a new American edition, which has been selling about 1,000 copies a month for about 18 months! It is actually the only book which I adored writing, because the people were so interesting, and it only took me just over a year to write. Normally I would say a book takes about three years for me to write. *The Savage God* took four years to write and got shorter and shorter.

My ambition now is to stop! There is an exchange I can't get out of my head, in *Pride and Prejudice*, when the daughter of the house is playing the piano for the assembled guests, and everyone claps politely, and she goes up to her mother and says, 'Shall I play another piece?' and her mother replies, 'Thank you darling, you have delighted us enough already.' I feel that is me; I have delighted you enough already! Unfortunately, though, writers don't have pensions, and so I can't afford to stop.

# Michael Bond

*Michael Bond began writing in 1945, when he was 19, and sold his first short story to a magazine. Surprisingly, he told me the story was a bit risqué. In any event, it made him decide that he wanted to be a writer. At first he wrote short stories and radio plays for adults. His first book for children,* A Bear Called Paddington, *in 1958, was followed by more, which were so successful he was able to give up a job as a cameraman at the BBC and write full time. The Paddington books alone have sold more than thirty million copies. Paddington is a household name of international repute with his own 'life-size' bronze statue at Paddington Station.*

When I was a child, although I loved being read to, I did not like reading. It was the Paddington Bear books which changed this. Much later I lived in Arundel Gardens in Notting Hill, very near where I always imagined Paddington to live, so I was extremely pleased to find out that Michael Bond had previously lived in a tiny flat in the same street. After interviewing him, Michael Bond wrote me a charming letter with the extract from his book which he chose to be quoted. But the opening of his letter deserves quotation too in its display of his affable nature and his complete belief in Paddington, which is why the books work so well and are so endearing. 'It was nice meeting you yesterday; all the more so for your past connection with Arundel Gardens. Paddington would have fallen over backwards with surprise. Perhaps it's a good job I was sitting down.'

Michael Bond now lives in a large house, but it is still not far from Paddington Station. When I visited, newspapers covered a table in the basement and a cutting from one, on top, was about a dog in Battersea Dogs' Home who had learnt to undo his door at night, let out all his friends and have a good time. The article might almost have been about Olga da Polga, and indeed there was a real guinea pig in a hutch, while *a tortoise was visible on the lawn outside. All around the rooms were various models and pictures of bears, and of Paddington in particular, although the actual bear who sparked off the stories was not at home.*

## Selected Bibliography

Children's Books
*A Bear Called Paddington* (1958), *More About Paddington* (1959), *Paddington Marches On* (1964), *Paddington Goes to Town* (1968), *Parsley's Good Deed* (Herbs Story Books, 1969), *Paddington Takes the Air* (1970), *Parsley the Lion* (1972), *The Tales of Olga da Polga* (1975), *Olga Meets Her Match* (1975), *Paddington Goes Out* (1980)

Adult Books
*Monsieur Pamplemousse* (1983), *Monsieur Pamplemousse Rests His Case* (1991), *Monsieur Pamplemousse Hits the Headlines* (2003)

When Michael Bond sent me this extract from *Paddington Helps Out*, he added a short introduction: 'Things sometimes get off to a bad start when Paddington is involved. Like the time the family had dinner at the Porchester in order to celebrate his birthday.'

'Well, Paddington,' said Mr. Brown. 'What would you like to start with? Soup? *Hors d'oevres*?'

Paddington looked at his menu in disgust. He didn't think much of it at all. 'I don't know what I would like, Mr Brown,' he said. 'My programme's full of mistakes and I can't read it.'

'*Mistakes!*' The head waiter raised one eyebrow to its full height and looked at Paddington severely. 'There is never a mistake on a Porchester menu.'

'Those aren't mistakes, Paddington,' whispered Judy, as she looked over his shoulder. 'It's French.'

'French!' exclaimed Paddington. 'Fancy printing a menu in French!'

Mr Brown hastily scanned his own card. 'Er ... have you anything suitable for a young bear's treat?' he asked.

'A young bear's treat?' repeated the head waiter haughtily. 'We pride ourselves there is nothing one cannot obtain at the Porchester.'

'In that case,' said Paddington, looking most relieved. 'I think I'll have a marmalade sandwich.'

\*      \*      \*

I first started writing when I was in the army, stationed in the desert in Egypt, with some time on my hands. I wrote a short story, and because I used to take a magazine called *London Opinion* at the time, I sent it to them, and to my amazement I got a letter back, saying they would accept the story and '*London Opinion* will pay Michael Bond seven guineas.' I couldn't find anyone to cash the cheque at the time! The army post office didn't want to know about it and nor did a local Arab trade agent I showed it to. Seven guineas was quite a lot in those days, but I sometimes wished I'd kept it and had it framed.

The story I got the cheque for was based on a person going into a Cairo nightclub and having a drink with a recruiting officer and getting inveigled into signing on for the army. It was slightly risqué. When it came out I had a letter from my mother saying, 'Congratulations, but we are a bit worried about you dear, and hope you are all right!' At around that time I read that Ernest

Hemingway was being paid seven shillings and sixpence a word! And that, combined with getting my first story published, made me think, 'Oh God, I want to be a writer.'

I wrote some more stories for *Men Only* and *London Opinion* and soon after I was demobbed and worked for the BBC, in the sound department at first. But at the same time I did some articles for the then *Manchester Guardian* on any subject I could think of. I did one about canal boats, and another about the first espresso coffee machines that were just coming into England. Then I got interested in writing radio plays.

I have always been very fond of France – a great Francophile – and I wrote the sort of plays where, for instance, there would be a young man going to stay in a small village in France where there is a statue of a beautiful girl and one night in the full moon it comes alive and they have an adventure. The editors would get back to me saying they liked it, but that they didn't do fantasy. Next I acquired an agent and he managed to sell six of my plays to Hong Kong radio for five guineas a time. So I was writing for that kind of market and I had still never thought of writing for children.

One day, on Christmas Eve, when I hadn't got my first wife very much in the way of presents and wanted a kind of stocking-filler, I happened to go into Selfridges. It was snowing and I went in partly to shelter. I went upstairs to the toy department, and this sounds rather like a sob story, because it was fairly empty, and there was just this one small bear left on one of the shelves. I hesitated and went away, but thought, 'No, it is rather nice', and I went back and bought it.

Because we lived near Paddington at the time, I had actually always wanted to use that as a name for a character. It sounds sort of solid and west London. I had written some short stories for BBC radio, and one was about a rather accident-prone uncle who I was going to call Uncle Paddington, but I called him Uncle Parkington, and kept the name Paddington, thinking, 'Maybe I will use it for something better one day.'

So we called the bear I bought Paddington. He was quite small and used to sit on the shelf. He is still around, but I share custody of him with my first wife. So he spends a few months with her and then a few months at home with me. In those days, I used to sit and think, 'What shall I write about?' – which never happens nowadays. I had a blank sheet of paper and a typewriter and knew that unless I put some words down, no one else was going to. So to get my mind working I started writing about this small bear. It caught my fancy and in no time at all I had my first chapter.

I wasn't thinking about writing for children or of writing a book, but I showed it to my wife and she liked it very much and asked, 'Why don't you do some more?' So on my days off I did a chapter a day for eight days and realized I had a book on my hands. I sent it to my agent, who liked it, although he spotted one mistake. I said that Paddington came from Africa. My agent wrote and told me that there weren't any bears in Africa, which made me rather ashamed of my lack of knowledge about bears. So I went to the library and looked up about them and found there were some still left in the Pyrenees and there are some in Peru. I thought Peru sounded far enough away that people wouldn't know too much about it. Then I thought if I made it Darkest Peru, 'darkest' sounds a bit mysterious, so I used that.

The book went the rounds of a number of publishers who didn't want it because they already had a bear, or it was the wrong length, or that kind of thing. Then it went to Collins and the editor there liked it very much. He gave it to William Collins, one of the old-fashioned publishers, who always took a keen interest in what he was selling, and expected everybody on his staff to have read all the books. It was very nice in those days. I was also very lucky in having Peggy Fortnum to illustrate the first books, because although I had an idea of what Paddington should look like, she went to London Zoo and looked at actual bears.

All sorts of things came together rather fortuitously. I knew that Winnie-the-Pooh ate honey, even though I hadn't read the book at that time. So I thought of something else sticky for Paddington to eat, and came up with marmalade. For a long time I used to get parcels sent to me with marmalade and rather a lot of smashed glass! I think it was fortunate that I hadn't read *Winnie-the-Pooh*; because it is such a strong book, I might well have made Paddington a toy bear. But I thought of Paddington as a real bear.

I wrote about Paddington while I was living in a one-room flat, with a cupboard for a kitchen, near the Portobello Road. Further along there is a street called Lansdowne Crescent, and I know the Browns' house, 32 Windsor Gardens, is, to me, just round the first bend. Because I wrote the first book very quickly, I was wearing a government surplus duffel coat at the time, so I gave Paddington a duffel coat to wear. I also had an old army bush hat, so I gave him that. That was important to Paddington because the hat was given to him by his uncle and it had holes in it. So when Paddington goes to the cinema and keeps his hat on and someone tells him take it off, he says, 'You can look through the holes.' Paddington would be dreadful to have around, really.

I also decided Paddington should have a suitcase. This may have been because the first book I read by myself was *The Swiss Family Robinson*. I read it again recently and didn't actually like it, because I thought the family terribly priggish, or the mother was, but I liked the fact that she always had a duffel bag with useful things in. But mainly the suitcase, and Paddington's label saying 'Please look after this bear' came about because of childhood memories of the war. I lived in Reading and we had some evacuees who stayed with us. They were from the East End of London and had never seen the country before. I remember them arriving on the station, and they all had a suitcase, or a bag, and they all had a label round their neck with their name on. I found it a terribly sad sight. All these small children were allowed just one small bag or suitcase with all their possessions. And then to have a label in case they got lost. So that is how it came about with Paddington.

I still think the saddest sight in the world is refugees. At that time the newsreels were full of pictures of French refugees pushing all their possessions in a pram. I see Mr Gruber, Paddington's friend, as being a Hungarian refugee. Although the Browns and Mrs Bird are very welcoming, I felt the story needed someone who would understand what it was like for Paddington to be living in a strange country. It gives them a special relationship. The Browns are really modelled on my parents, I realized afterwards. If my mother had found a bear on Paddington Station she would have wanted to take it home if it was lost.

My father, who was a very nice, polite man, was very law-abiding and might have been more worried. For instance, where I was brought up, on an estate, there was a bus stop by some grass. Everyone used to take a short cut to the bus stop through the grass, but because there was a sign saying 'Please keep off the grass' my father would always walk round, along the path. So my father also has some of Paddington's characteristics and he also always wore a hat, which is another reason why I gave Paddington one. My father wore his hat in case he met someone he knew and had nothing to raise. I have got pictures of him on seaside holidays wearing his hat in the sea when he was going paddling! Paddington, like my father, is basically a very polite character. I find the sad thing in life nowadays is that there is so little politeness left. You can stand inside Selfridges and hold the door open all day and no one even looks at you.

Anyway, the first book got on some so-called 'best-seller lists' and did very well, so Collins wanted another one. So without meaning to, I suddenly found myself being a children's author, although I don't really distinguish between being a writer for children or adults. Obviously there are parameters that you don't go beyond with children's books, and while I am writing a picturebook, I do have to write most of it within the experience of a small child – like going to the supermarket and that sort of thing, although I have occasionally used quite sophisticated situations. Like when Paddington bought some dud shares in the market, and I think children still probably understood it. And sometimes adults can explain things to the child. I think reading is a shared experience and if the person reading the story is enjoying it, that communicates itself to the child.

But I write not for an imagined audience, but to please myself. I have had trouble with America, who have lists of words they don't use, and I think it is a shame. I have just turned down something because they wanted to change so much. But I feel that you don't want to use the same words that any other character might use. So long as a word is clear in the context, I see no reason not to use it. I think children hate being written down to and are much more intelligent than we give them credit for.

The easiest things with books is dialogue. If I get Paddington into a situation with some official who is being a bit pompous, the book starts to write itself. I find the act of moving characters around from room to room is often harder. You can easily write 'she walked out of the room', but really there should be some reason for it, other than that you want to get rid of her at that point and have no dialogue for her. I think I am particularly aware of that from having worked in television when I kept hearing actors ask, 'Why am I doing this?'

All the things I have written since Paddington are character-driven. I think if you know the character and put him into a situation, things develop. Up until then I think I had been writing stories that were plot-driven and then I tried to put characters in, and they never really came alive. I feel if the author doesn't believe in his characters, why should anybody else? Also, as I said, beforehand I would get things returned because editors said they didn't publish fantasy, and yet no one ever said that about Paddington. But a talking bear living in Notting Hill Gate is pure fantasy!

No one in the books ever says, 'Oh gosh, a talking bear!' – they are not surprised. He is accepted. I think it may be because he can somehow be relied upon to react in a certain way. He doesn't really change. I think a lot of people are rather envious of

Paddington's lifestyle. He has got one or two good friends who he sees on his own terms, and in the evening, if he would rather be on his own, he says, 'Oh, I think I'll go upstairs and do my accounts.' And nobody queries it.

The actor Peter Bull, who used to collect bears, said, 'Whereas dolls are always wondering what they are going to wear next, you never quite know what bears are thinking, but you feel you can trust them with your secrets.' There is that quality about them, and I think children tell bears things they wouldn't necessarily tell their parents. So it is a strange quality because bears in the wild are not the friendliest of creatures.

If you put Paddington in a situation, you know it is going to go wrong, and the readers are split down the middle: half want to say, 'No, don't do it' and the other half want him to do it to see how he will get out of trouble. The difficult thing with writing Paddington is how to end it so that if he wrecks the joint, somebody benefits by it. It might be that he has papered over all the walls and the door and shut himself in, as he did do, and then it turns out Mrs Brown wanted that room redone anyway. I think right should triumph over wrong and someone should benefit. So the most difficult thing about the Paddington stories is often getting the twist at the end. To me the stories are partly a mathematical problem, requiring an enticing start and a satisfying end.

Paddington thinks laterally and can't understand the strange complications human beings make for themselves. I remember going past a café in Haslemere, where I lived at the time, which said, 'Closed for lunch'. I just walked on, but Paddington would immediately think, 'But you can't be closed for lunch!' So ideas for Paddington often come about through simple things like that. I am a great believer in the subconscious doing work – you feed some ideas in, and some weeks later when a few things have come together, you think, 'There is a story there.' Similarly, if Paddington was watching tennis, and somebody called out 'deuce' he would think, 'Where's the juice? I want some. Why does he keep saying that if there isn't any juice?' Sometimes Paddington makes me laugh when I am working because he comes out with something I wasn't expecting myself. As far as I am concerned you do need a total belief in the character you are writing about, and then it does kind of take over.

After I had written several books about Paddington I had to decide whether to stay in television as a cameraman, or to give it up and write full time. I decided to do full-time writing and left, and then suddenly realized there is a cold hard world outside. I wanted to get a mortgage and suddenly I was free-lance. But it was only two or three weeks after I had left the BBC that the head of children's programmes rang me up and asked if I had any ideas for *Children's Hour*. At that time they were doing away with things like *Bill and Ben the Flowerpot Men* and revamping the programme.

It so happened that I had been looking out of the window and saw some parsley blowing in the wind, which I thought looked a bit like a lion's mane. So I said, 'Well I've got an idea for a possible story.' Next I had to have a script, so I rushed down to the public library and got Culpepper's *Complete Herbal*. Practically every herb suggested itself as a character if you read the description of it. For instance, basil suggested a rather aristocratic tall figure, so I decided on Sir Basil and Lady Rosemary. Dill became a dog and there was Constable Knapweed, and I wrote a script for *Watch With Mother*, which were quarter-hour programmes.

They liked it, and I went up to see them, and they asked how I saw it being done. At that time, around 1968, they wanted to get rid of marionettes. I was actually very keen on puppets, because when I was small I used to build myself marionette theatres. But I said, 'I don't really see The Herbs as glove puppets, so I am not sure'. It was around the time that *The Magic Roundabout*, using stop-motion animation, had been bought by the BBC, and they said, 'There is someone living in France, called Ivor Wood, an animator and director, who worked on *The Magic Roundabout*, and maybe he could do something similar.' So I met Ivor Wood and we had a chat and he came back with some models and *The Herbs* took off from there.

We did 13 programmes. It was very easy as the writer. I could just say, 'Mr and Mrs Onion march on, followed by 12 Chives' which might take a few seconds to type, but would be a day's work for an animator. The two leading characters were Parsley and Dill, who were a bit like Morecambe and Wise, and they, too, used to write themselves, in a way. I used to get up in the morning and think, 'It's Friday/Flyday' and an idea would come about aeroplanes and I could write the first script by, say, 11 am, and then do a rewrite, and it was just a morning's work.

In those days I had an old-fashioned typewriter. I tried one again the other day and I couldn't make the keys hit the page! You forget how easy and light it is with a computer. But then, I would do five carbon copies, or whatever, and not make mistakes, because it was a lot of work to alter. Now, using a computer, I can't type a complete sentence without a mistake because it is so easy to correct. I do a lot of rewriting now, because I find something is never finished now. But I think computers are wonderful. You get up and switch them on and you have got words before you. You don't ever have that completely blank sheet of paper! But as soon as I start writing, I also start altering slightly.

I work every day (I have even worked on Christmas Day) but do most of my writing in the morning. I like leaving off when I could go on, because then I can start the next day. I set myself targets and if I have done three of four pages, I consider that a good day's work and would stop there. I don't think I write as quickly as I did at one time, but then that may be because of all the rewriting. Whether it is better or not I am not sure, but I tell myself it is.

Altogether I have written about 100 stories about Paddington in 13 books. I didn't want it to get stale, or feel I was scraping the barrel, so I started doing stories for younger children and they caught on. I wrote *Olga da Polga* because my daughter had a guinea pig. They were more of a challenge, because although Paddington has got his feet firmly on the ground – he is not the sort of bear who would ever go to the moon or anything like that – he has the territory of Notting Hill Gate and he gets about, but Olga's world is inside a house. So she is not such a nice character as Paddington because she has to use the other characters, like the cat and the tortoise, in order to have adventures.

Guinea pigs are lovely pets. The one we have downstairs now rules the roost really. In fact I started making a live-action television film some years ago. But trying to capture a guinea pig on film isn't really on. I wrote a story, but animals just do what they want to do, and so there is an awful lot of wasted film, which is very expensive. The guinea pig we have now, I think would quite enjoy being filmed, and I'm sure would tell me what exposure she should be on, but the one we had at the time would go into her bedroom and hide as soon as I came near the hutch.

Paddington was very lucky when he went on the television. Several people had a go, usually with someone dressed up in a bearskin, which was totally hopeless. And Paddington is quite a slow-moving character, not suited to cartoons. But Ivor Wood, who always thought things out very carefully, said, 'I think it would be worth making a pilot of Paddington with one three-dimensional bear and cardboard cut-outs.' He used muted backgrounds and Paddington was the only really colourful character, and it was the only television adaptation that worked really well. Even that was destroyed gradually because it was sold to America. They didn't really understand it, and wanted all the backgrounds made brighter and the cardboard cut-outs to have lip sync which couldn't work, and so I said 'No' to any more of those.

When he was on television I went through a period when everybody wanted Paddington merchandise – some of it dreadful, like a wastepaper bucket with Paddington's head on top which you lifted up – so that was a definite 'No'. But if ever I had any doubt as to whether it was good or bad, I used to think, 'What would Paddington think of it?' and if I felt he wouldn't like it, I would say so.

I know that when the original stuffed Paddington Bears came out, my daughter (who was born the year the first book was published) was at the age when she just wanted to be herself. She was always being introduced at parties as 'the daughter of Michael Bond, who writes the Paddington books'. It wasn't that she disliked Paddington, she just wanted to be herself. But when she left school, I took her down to university in Exeter, and when we got there there were girls arriving and a lot of them had their Paddington Bears with them, and I said, 'There is no escape!' She got used to it, but I felt for her at the time. But the bears did sell mostly to girls going out into the world, getting their first flat, and they wanted a kind of father figure in the corner. It wasn't a kind of cuddly toy because it was quite solid.

In Japan, Paddington used to be the mascot for one of the banks and all the tellers would have a Paddington Bear standing by them. There was also a Paddington Bear credit card for women only, for whatever reason, in Japan. Some people take Paddington very seriously. Once I was signing books and a man who obviously worked in the City, with a bowler hat that they used to wear in those days, asked me to sign an old passport for him. He had taken out his own photograph and put Paddington's in. He said, 'Everywhere I go in the world, I get this stamped!'

I went on a signing tour of Australia a few years ago, and I had to take a Paddington Bear with me wherever I went. And almost each time I got on a plane I would get a message from the captain asking if Paddington could go up and see the flight deck. So I would take him up, and once the captain said, 'Do you mind if he stays here?' So I left him, strapped into a seat, and later got a message saying, 'Do you mind if Paddington stays till the end as he would like to land the plane?'

I used to get lots of letters about Paddington, but I don't get so many now, because people don't write letters so much and I don't give my email address out. Recently there was an article in a collectors' magazine where they valued autographs, and mine was valued at around £60 or £70. Suddenly I got loads of letters saying things like, 'I loved Paddington as a child, and so do my six children. Could you send them each a signed photograph?' Another woman wrote three times. I always reply to anyone who is genuine, but you can't to all those. In fact there is a company who supply people with a kit for getting autographs. It is always a letter on lined paper, with a recycled envelope enclosed, and they always say the same thing, beginning 'Dear Michael', which irritates me.

But of all the stories I have written, the Paddington ones have brought me a lot of pleasure. I had one letter from a nun who was suffering some terrible disease and she wrote, 'Thank you very much for Paddington, because he has given me so much comfort.' I also remember having quite a long letter from a boy in Canada, who wasn't complaining at all, but reading between the lines, I think his mother was probably a prostitute and his father drank. He ended up talking about his dog, saying unfortunately it only had three legs! It painted a terrible picture, but he thanked me for the Paddington books and said he wished he had a bear like him. That kind of thing always gives me pleasure, because it is like an unsolicited hug.

Another nice time I had was when I was in a restaurant in the City that had booths. I was by myself and I could hear two men in the next booth talking about Paddington and roaring with laughter remembering various stories. I didn't go round and tell them I was there because it would have spoilt it. It was nice because you rarely get that sort of feedback. I mean relatives are bound to say they like it. I am still surprised how successful Paddington became. If I go into bookshops I don't look to see if they are on the shelves because if they are, you think, 'Oh God they haven't been sold', and if they are not, you think, 'Oh dear they are not stocking them.' I was cured of that early on when I couldn't see any in a shop so I asked if they had any, and the lady opened a cupboard and got one out – they were just waiting to go on the shelves – so I had to buy one!

Now I spend most of my time writing the adult books about the French detective Monsieur Pamplemousse. I have finished the fifteenth and am just thinking about number sixteen. As with Paddington, I put the character into a situation, not knowing what is going to happen, and things develop because of the sort of character he is. I like to go to France to see if there is somewhere to set a story.

Some years ago I went to a place near Bordeaux, a part I had never been to before. There were some enormous sand dunes, the biggest in Europe, but I couldn't really see anything to write about. But that winter there were huge gales and there was a picture in the paper of those sand dunes where a lot of sand had blown away and revealed a buried German tank. That suddenly clicked in my mind and from that started a story. Most of those stories seem to develop that way. The one I have just finished is about terrorism, which is quite difficult to be funny about, and in fact I nearly abandoned it halfway through. But I think it has worked out all right. It is a plot to inject poison into the food chain.

And I might soon be writing another Paddington book for his fiftieth anniversary. Paddington is still very much a part of my life. If I met him in the street, he would probably raise his hat, and I would nod, because I haven't got one, and we would probably go our separate ways. It is a bit like believing in something like Father Christmas: your common sense tells you that such a person doesn't exist, but you still perpetuate the myth for small children. But Paddington is real to me.

# Raymond Briggs

*Raymond Briggs, author/illustrator and master of the strip-cartoon format, left school at 15, in 1949, to study painting at Wimbledon School of Art. This was followed by two years of national service before attending the Slade School of Art. His first work was in advertising, but he soon won acclaim as an illustrator. In order to earn more, Briggs decided to write as well as illustrate, often basing his characters on his family – his milkman father and his mother who had been a lady's maid. Briggs has won numerous awards and international renown.*

*There can be very few people, adults or children, who do not have some knowledge of* The Snowman *– a wordless book told with over 150 pictures. In England the animated film has become an institution shown on television every Christmas along with older stalwarts such as Bing Crosby's* White Christmas. The Snowman *embodies what is common in Briggs' work: the relationship between a child and a magical being in the real world. But* The Snowman *was created deliberately to contrast Briggs' previous book* Fungus the Bogeyman *and is one of his most gentle stories. In other books, while there is tenderness and humour, there is also the element (possibly an influence from the fairy tales and nursery rhymes Briggs loves) of the macabre, sad or surreal, with themes of the underdog, the working classes and almost Pinteresque servant/ master relationships.*

## Selected Bibliography

Children's Books
*Peter and the Piskies* (illustrator, 1958), *Midnight Adventure* (1961), *The Mother Goose Treasury* (illustrator, 1966), *Jim and the Beanstalk* (1970), *Father Christmas* (1973), *Fungus the Bogeyman* (1977),

*The Snowman* (1978), *Gentleman Jim* (1980), *The Man* (1992), *The Bear* (1994), *The Puddleman* (2004)

Adult Illustrated Books
*When the Wind Blows* (1982), *Ethel and Ernest* (1998)

From *The Man*: This is an argument that occurs late in the book between the man (in bold) and John. It was chosen by Briggs in part, because it is one of the few examples of dialogue not contained within speech bubbles or dependent on illustration:

I like watching you eat.

**Do you?**

Yes.

**You like watching me eat. You like watching me drink. How would you like to be watched all the time? I'm not on stage! I'm not an actor! This is me! This is MY LIFE! I don't want you turning it into a PERFORMANCE! Go and watch the telly if you want entertainment! Don't watch ME! I REFUSE TO BE ENTERTAINMENT! I AM ME!**

I like that! I've been like a mother to you. I've cooked for you! Bathed you! Clothed you! Cleaned up your babyish messes!

**Don't try and be noble! You enjoyed it! You were fascinated! You weren't being kind. You weren't being generous. You were PLAYING! Playing with a NEW TOY! I will not be anyone's TOY!**

\*        \*        \*

I am supposed to be quite good at doing dialogue – at least various people have told me that I am. I do almost nothing but dialogue – I don't think I have practically ever written any continuous prose. Most of my books are in strip-cartoon form, which is rather like writing a script for a film. It is the same with the biography of my mother and father, *Ethel and Ernest*: that is told entirely in dialogue without a single word of narration apart from dates and days of the week. But it is really the way that I illustrate that leads to that sort of writing.

People don't always realize that you have a set number of pages in a picturebook – usually 32, although occasionally you are allowed 40 or 48 on very rare occasions – it has got to be a multiple of eight because of the way the paper is folded to make the pages. When I was writing *Father Christmas*, back in 1973, I realized I needed far more than 32 pictures, so I had to do four, five, six pictures a page, and sometimes 10 or almost 20 a page. So I was actually forced into doing strip-cartoon, which is a nightmare form to work in because it is so laborious and there are so many pictures to do. In strip-cartoon you *can* have a tiny bit of narration, but I don't seem to do that.

I find I quite enjoy it because the pictures are telling what is physically going on. You don't have to say, 'The man came into the room and said . . . ' because there is a picture of him doing it, so dialogue makes the writing part quicker, and comes naturally to me.

Physically, however, it is still very slow. I usually hand-write all the dialogue. Nowadays you can write out your own alphabet in both lower case and capitals and this can be set into a computer and the person then types it out and it is all composed in your hand-lettering. But you have still got to do the layout of each speech bubble, so I don't feel it really helps. You would either have to design the bubble so the typist can lay it out exactly, or you would have to get the operator to type it all out as a script and then physically cut it all up, making up the lines for the bubble. And then of course you would have to go back to the typist each time you wanted to make an alteration, unless you did it all yourself. But if you are hand-lettering it, you just stick a piece of paper over the top and redo it, which is much simpler.

When I first started, the only thing I was trying to achieve was to earn a living – that was my main obsession. I thought I couldn't possibly go to art school for six bloody years, plus two in the army, and then at the end not earn a living from what I had been doing. At art school we were all dragooned into being painters, although I originally went there wanting to be a cartoonist. But I was told that was not an occupation for a gentleman: it was rather looked-down upon. So I was pushed into painting and did four years at Wimbledon and then went on to the Slade to do two more years of fine-art painting, constantly being told that commercial art was *infra dig*. But I was determined to earn a living and you couldn't with painting in those days. So I tried doing illustrating.

There are three sorts of illustrating one can do: advertising, magazines and books. I found I liked books the best although they were the worst paid – advertising was the best paid, but awful work, and magazines were better paid than books, but rather ghastly subject matter. So I decided on books, but then to my horror, realized that books meant children's books, which I wasn't really remotely interested in! But gradually I got interested, and found there was marvellous stuff, like nursery rhymes, to illustrate. I still think nursery rhymes and fairy tales are the finest things in the world from the illustrator's point of view. I was also doing a lot of fairly routine short novels or texts written by other authors, and I thought some of them were so badly written that I could do better myself!

I did one just for fun, and showed it to the editor, hoping to get some advice on how to proceed as a writer, but to my absolute *amazement* he said he would publish it. I thought, 'It just shows the standard! Someone with no training and knowing nothing can get a book published.' It was called *The Strange House*. Then

I did one or two more of those, but I had fallen in love with nursery rhymes, and so next I did a series of nursery rhymes. The American publisher who did them said she wanted to do the world's biggest and best nursery rhyme collection – I think it was 800 illustrations and hundreds of rhymes, and that was *The Mother Goose Treasury.*

But having written one or two of my own books, it eventually dawned on me that from the money-earning point of view, you got paid a royalty as an author, which you don't as an illustrator, although the illustrator does about ten times more work on a book than the author. So I finally realized, after several years, that the best thing to do was one's own picturebooks. You have the freedom, the colour, the space, and can write your own text and get paid a royalty.

In my case the story and the pictures are all mixed up. I don't draw many of the pictures in advance, because I can see them in my head anyway. It is more like writing a film, with a rough sort of storyboard. You might have a dummy blank picture-book, and write the text in that. But the writing, the illustration and the design all go hand in hand, at the same time. Each spread [a double page] is a kind of chapter. You usually have to end a sequence at the bottom of a right-hand page and move on to another sequence, like a cut in a film, or a chapter in a written book.

First I lay everything out in pencil, then make a dummy of the book, and photocopy the artwork and paste it in to send to the publisher, so they see the layout, design, text and illustration together. Then you have to draw up the actual spreads on water-colour paper or whatever you are using and add coloured crayon to the pencil drawings. Usually, as I said, I use hand-lettering, although with *The Man* I had it typeset. I had a lot of help from the designer at Walker Books with that, and she helped work out the three different typefaces. I try to do as few roughs as possible, because you are emptying the tank all the time.

In *The Puddleman* the little boy appears 81 times. When I had nearly finished, I decided he should be wearing wellingtons instead of shoes. This meant rubbing out 162 shoes and drawing 162 wellingtons. After that, I thought he should be in shorts, not jeans, so 81 pairs of shorts had to be changed! Illustration takes so long that you are doing it throughout the day. Writing is relatively quick. Allan Alberg said he had an idea for a picturebook one morning and wrote it in a day, and his wife spent the next year illustrating it! You can write a sentence saying, 'The princess, the dwarf, the king, the three little gnomes, the cow and the bull all ran down the street.' That is done and finished, but if you have to illustrate that, it is about two weeks' work, quite apart from researching what cows look like, running, and what medieval costume is like, or whatever.

I do the books because I get haunted by this blasted idea hanging around, that I can't quite formulate, but when it goes well, it is very nice, particularly bits of dialogue. I often think of bits of dialogue in the middle of the night. For instance, with *When the Wind Blows*, which was the one that carried me away more than most, I would wake up in the middle of the night and switch on the light and write down two or three lines of dialogue. 'He could say . . . and she could say . . . ' If you don't write it down, of course you go to sleep and forget it, so you just bung it down. That is the sort of thing that is good. And sometimes you laugh out loud at your own jokes if something is funny.

A lot of my stories are fairly class-based: it is me talking to my father. You have got an educated, potentially middle-class youngster, talking to a rougher, tougher, less educated, working-class man. That is what *The Man* is all about, and some of the others are a bit that way. There is often that sort of a relationship, and a kind of tension between them because of that, but also a great affection or love.

*The Puddleman* is very closely based on my surrogate grandson. It all came from him, which is why the book is dedicated to him. He calls me Collar, and puts a thing on my wrist and takes me out for walks and bosses me about. It was his idea to give the puddles names, and he also said, '*They* haven't put any puddle in that one!' It was wonderful, and he was scarcely four at the time. I was immediately given two brilliant surreal concepts. 'They' meant person or persons unknown put the puddles in, and 'puddle' is a substance in its own right – nothing to do with water. That was the basis of the whole idea. I haven't often got ideas from children, but I am basing another book, at the moment, on things this little chap I get on so well with has come up with.

Earlier on, when *his* father was a youngster, I wrote *Gentleman Jim*, which was based on a conversation I had when he said, 'When I grow up, I don't want to go to work, I want to live in a cave in the woods and catch rabbits and have camp fires.' I rather stupidly pointed out that you can't live on other people's land because there are laws about trespass and the rabbits all belong to someone, and you are not allowed to light fires in a public place. That gave me the idea of thinking about what would happen if an adult with the mind of a ten year old tried to put his concepts into practice. Little boys want to be cowboys, well, supposing he actually thought, 'I'm going to be a cowboy. I must buy a gun and get to Texas!' Then you come up against this wall of lack of education, lack of money and of course bureaucracy above all.

*Father Christmas* is based on my father who was a milkman. My father delivered milk in the cold and Father Christmas delivers presents. And Father Christmas's house is closely based on the house I grew up in. That occurs again in *Ethel and Ernest*: the old sink and the wooden draining board. Occasionally things turn up, and I write for adults rather than children, as I did again with *When the Wind Blows* [which is about an elderly couple preparing for, and living through, a nuclear war]. You don't think who the book is for while you are doing it, you just have an idea and get on with it. Often you have practically got to the end before you know whether it is a children's book or not.

I don't see much difference actually. Once the child can read fluently at the age of seven or eight if they are bright, they can read practically anything. It is only the subject matter they are not interested in. They are not interested in sex, or high finance, or crime. One of the great things about strip-cartoon is that it does invite the reluctant reader in. If they are confronted with columns of grey text, they might think, 'Oh no! It's like school.' But when they pick up something that looks like a comic, they get intrigued, and don't realize they are reading quite long, difficult words.

Of course *The Snowman* is a book without any words. I had written *Fungus the Bogeyman* just before, and was sick to death of all those words and slime and muck, and I thought I must do something nice and simple and clean and easy. I had had it in the file to do for six years – these things hang around for years because you can think of an idea in an instant and jot it down. *Fungus* took over two years, and *Ethel and Ernest* over three years, so other ideas are hanging about. I was very pleased *The Snowman* took off to such a degree, though I am getting slightly fed up with it because it is so enormous now – people don't realize quite how big, because you don't see so much of it in this country. But only this very morning, I was asked to write an introduction to The Snowman Fan Club in Japan – Oh God! It is difficult to do, because what the hell do you say?

I have written pieces about the Isle of Man stamps, because the Snowman is used there this year, and on the Isle of Man 50p coin – Britain's first coin ever with colour on it. It goes on and on: it is just bizarre. There was a whole Snowman convention held in Stoke-on-Trent, at a factory, where people come for two or three days, and have lectures and talks and buy the new editions of the figurines they have made, and talk to the modellers and talk to the designers, and auction collectables. It is a mini industry: there is an office in London that does nothing else! The book did get awards all over the world, so it would have been a sort of best-seller, but without the film, I don't know if it would have kept in print every year for 30 years.

You do not expect a film of a children's story to be the same as the book. For one thing, there is not enough material in the book to make a film. As I said, a picturebook is 32 pages long, and that would last about six minutes on a film, and *The Snowman* was a 26-minute film. So they had to expand the story, and other people extend it and write it. I remember when the producer rang me and said, 'We are thinking of having them fly off, not just to Brighton Pier, but to the North Pole and meet Father Christmas.' I thought, 'Oh God, no! Really, how corny can you get?' But actually it works very well and wouldn't be the proper film without it. So that was good. Some other films made of my books I haven't liked very much, but *When the Wind Blows* was quite a good film.

I am quite pleased with *When the Wind Blows* because it made such a *stupendous* impression at the time. There was the film, of course, and I did a radio play of it, which won an award. There was also a stage play which was at the Whitehall Theatre, just around the corner from old mother Thatcher, and it was in every paper, and mentioned in the House of Lords and the House of Commons. I did over 200 interviews about it, all round the country – it was just endless. I don't know what has made some things so successful: I don't like to think about it. My favourite book is *Ethel and Ernest*, because it is about my mum and dad and home.

You don't have much of a future when you are 70, but I am doing a whacking great Ted Hughes at the moment. It is a great honour to do it, but a bit oppressive – a massive job at this age. It is nine volumes of his poems collected into one, and muggins is illustrating it, which is wonderful to do, but a bit huge. I am not complaining, but I shan't do another job of this size. I have worked out about 290 illustrations, which is an awful lot, and I will have to cut down on that. But it is a great honour to be doing it at all.

I also did a whole load of stuff for the Royal Mail earlier this year. It was supposed to be just six stamps, but then they asked me to do the aerogramme letter, and the presentation sheet, and this and that and the other. So that was a big job that lasted months and months. So actually, just as I am trying to calm down, I get the two biggest and most prestigious jobs I have ever done: stamps for the Royal Mail, and collected Ted Hughes! But I still want to do my own picturebooks. I get bugged by an idea. It is like a niggle, and you do it to get rid of this irritant. You have this idea annoying you, and the only way to deal with it, like scratching an itch really, is to get it down and get it out. Then you are free of it, thank God!

# Tracy Chevalier

*Tracy Chevalier is a young, successful, modest, frank writer of historical fiction. Born in 1962, she grew up in Washington, DC, but after graduating in Ohio she moved to England and has stayed ever since, living with her husband and son in London. She loved books as a child, and wrote a couple of stories in her teens, but it was only when she left her job as a reference book editor and took an MA in creative writing at the University of East Anglia that she started to write seriously.*

*Chevalier began* The Virgin Blue *at University, when she considered that she finally had an idea 'big' enough to fill a novel. The idea for her second novel developed when lying in bed studying the face in a poster of the Vermeer painting 'Girl With a Pearl Earring', which had hung in her bedroom since she was 19. Within three days she had the story worked out. The book (with the same title) has sold over two million copies and was made into a stunning film.*

*Critics have admired Chevalier's telling details, evocative images and haunting poignancy, the* Independent *claiming she 'gives the kiss of life to the historical novel'. Tracy Chevalier has a great website (www.tchevalier.com) where she openly discusses possible flaws in her work, lists books she has enjoyed reading, and answers questions about her life, research and interpretations of her books. Unusually with writers, she is also happy to talk about her work in progress.*

## Selected Bibliography

Novels
*The Virgin Blue* (1997), *Girl With a Pearl Earring* (1999), *Falling Angels* (2001), *The Lady and the Unicorn* (2003)

From the opening of *Girl With a Pearl Earring*:

> My mother did not tell me they were coming. Afterwards she said she did not want me to appear nervous. I was surprised, for I thought she knew me well. Strangers would think I was calm. I did not cry as a baby. Only my mother would note the tightness along my jaw, the widening of my already wide eyes.
>
> I was chopping vegetables in the kitchen when I heard voices outside our front door – a woman's, bright as polished brass, and a man's, low and dark like the wood of the table I was working on. They were the kind of voices we heard rarely in our house. I could hear rich carpets in their voices, books and pearls and fur.
>
> I was glad that earlier I had scrubbed the front step so hard.

*     *     *

This passage is descriptive in a very particular way that I tend to favour. Not the long, Victorian descriptions of landscape and the minutiae of people's faces, the way, say, George Eliot or Jane Austen would do – in mine, the first thing you learn about the people coming to the house is what their voices are like. So it is looking at something from a slightly unusual angle, and the way the voices are described is very much grounded in everyday objects, because the voices are heard by the girl. I try to never have my characters think or speak out of character. The metaphors that this particular character would use are very much part of the education, or lack of education, or kind of life she would have. So it is about brass and wood – two things that she would know. If you use the third person, you can have a more knowing gaze. But I wanted this book, in particular, to be from the girl's point of view, because so much has been written about Vermeer's point of view, and nothing about, or from, hers. I wanted everything to be seen through her eyes. But that presents a certain set of limitations because she is limited in what she has seen in the world.

Another thing I tend to do in my writing is to emphasize the different senses. In describing voices as something very concrete, like brass and wood, it underpins everything you think about those characters later on. Throughout the book Catharina becomes quite brassy, and I tend to see her in yellow, with blonde hair, and there is a clashy brightness about her. Vermeer is described as dark wood, and it is not just that there is a lot of dark wood in those houses, but I wanted people to think of him as slightly impenetrable. I always thought of him as a cello, so it refers to that a bit too. These slightly oblique descriptions of people give you things to play with in your head.

Colour is very important to me. It used to be unconscious, although since so many people have pointed it out to me, it is starting to become conscious! I think in part, it is because since most of my characters are set in the past, I have to find some common ground between us and them, and for me, colour and the senses are one way. We may have different views on religion, or society now, but the sun still shines on someone now as it did then; bread still smells the same. These are ways of making the past less foreign to us. I emphasize the visual a lot. It is probably because the way I write is to see a scene in my head and write down what I see. Colour and light comes into that a lot – it is almost like a private film and the colour is really important to me. I am also constantly stimulated by visual things, and so I write about things I have seen.

I usually start with an image, like the picture of *Girl With a Pearl Earring*, or Highgate Cemetery in *Falling Angels*, or the tapestries in *The Lady and the Unicorn*. Sometimes people say that that image is almost like another character in the book, which

I think is very true. Then I do a lot of research about that specific thing, so I read a lot about Vermeer, and about tapestry weaving. As I am reading, I start coming up with the characters. After that the plot comes. Sometimes I know the ending, like with *Girl With a Pearl Earring*, I knew that the painting was going to be painted, so I was really working backwards from that. But in *The Virgin Blue*, my first novel to be published, I wasn't sure what the ending was going to be for a long time.

I first started writing short stories in my 20s. None were historical: they were all slices of contemporary life, and even now, when I am commissioned to write short stories by magazine editors, it is always that. It is funny, because I think they imagine they are going to get a mini *Girl With a Pearl Earring* and then I turn in something *completely* different. People have asked if I am going to collect my short stories, but, no. Although I am adequate, and know how to put a short story together, nothing really *sings*.

The University of East Anglia course was very good for me in that it made me have a different kind of life. I had been an editor in a publishing company of reference books. For a time I tried to fit my writing around that, but the course turned the equation round completely, so writing became the centre of my life. Other people might just quit their job and start writing, but I felt I needed the legitimacy of a course to allow me to do it. I had been writing at night and at weekends, and sometimes it would take me a long time to get around to it, but on the course, for a year, I was writing all the time. I had a love/hate relationship with that. No writer sits down to their blank piece of paper every day with great relish – sometimes, but not always. It also gave me a year to think, and work things out. I wrote some short stories during that year, but during the second half, I had the idea for *The Virgin Blue* and I started expanding that and started writing, at least the contemporary section, while I was at UEA. After I graduated I did freelance editing and would write in the morning and edit in the afternoon, and *The Virgin Blue* got written that way.

I have been very lucky with the publishing process. One of my peers, Martin Bedford, on the UEA course, had finished a novel and sent it to Curtis Brown Agency, to the slushpile of unsolicited manuscripts. But an assistant there, called Jonny Geller, was helping one of the agents by digging around the slushpile and he found my friend's manuscript. He read it and said, 'Oh, this is good!' and he asked his boss if he could take a crack at selling it, and his boss said, 'Sure'. So he sold it at an auction for something like £100,000 – it was this really huge deal, and they very quickly made him an agent, although he only had one client!

When I found out about this, I wrote to Jonny Geller and said, 'I've just finished a novel, and I am a friend of Martin's, could you do the same for me please?' And because he had no clients, he was eager to read, and so he read *The Virgin Blue* in a day, and got back to me saying he would represent me! Of course he didn't do the huge deal that my friend got, but nevertheless, he was quickly able to get a publisher and it was all very smooth. I was incredibly lucky because Jonny Geller is wonderful, and has become a real top agent now, very highly respected, and we get on so well, and he has been great with me. But it was really luck, because I know how hard it is to get the attention of an agent at all.

One thing about UEA, whether it is justified or not, is that it sets you slightly apart from the other hundreds of slushpile people. Agents are always looking for something that sets you apart, and if they have to look through 20 manuscripts that have arrived that day to read, and they see that one person has done a creative writing course at UEA, they think, 'Ah, well, someone must have thought they were pretty good, because they let them on that course.' I have to say that some of the writers on that course were *awful*, so it may not be legitimate, but it does help.

I would never have predicted that I would write about the past – it was an accident at first. *The Virgin Blue* was a real learning experience for me. When I had the idea to write that book I was just becoming more interested in my own family history for a variety of personal reasons. [In the book, the American heroine living in present-day France is drawn to investigate her ancestry.] It was in 1993/4, and I was pretty clear in my mind that I was going to remain in England, probably for the rest of my life. I was going to get married; my husband is English and I felt no real compelling reason to go back to the States. So I sometimes wonder if I wasn't looking for a link to root myself in Europe more than I had done. My father was born in Switzerland and in 1993 there was a family reunion there, and I met lots of my relatives, and it started me becoming much more interested in the Chevalier history.

So *The Virgin Blue* is partially biographical. I used to hate it when people asked me that before, although now I don't mind so much. I think that while I was writing the book, Ella was not meant to be me, but clearly, retrospectively, I can see that she sounds a lot like me. Writing the book [which tells the story in alternating chapters of two women, born centuries apart but bound by an ancestral legacy], I found the contemporary sections very easy, and originally the book was going to be mostly contemporary with just a few historical sections.

In fact the historical parts are shorter and more sparely written, but I think they have equal emotional impact. But I found writing the contemporary sections was almost too easy, too much like emotional diarrohoea. Whilst writing that part I didn't filter it, or consider it, and wasn't objective enough; I just let it come out. On the other hand, I had to write the historical sections much more carefully, and it forced me in some ways to be more sophisticated about how I wrote and how I thought about the past. And I discovered that as hard and as challenging as that was, I actually preferred it to writing in the present.

In some ways as well, it is an escape from myself. When I write it is such a joy, because I don't have to think about my own life. It is not that I have a bad life or anything, it is just that I live it every day, and writing about the past forces me to consider the broader world. That is another reason why I chose to write first-person narratives. I not only think about the past, but get into the mind of someone living then. In fact I am struggling now, because my next novel is about William Blake, and I have decided that I am going to write it in the third person, which is something I have never done very successfully.

Funnily enough the historical section of *The Virgin Blue* is in the third person, but everything else has been first person. And I have *tried*. The first draft of *Falling Angels* was, for the most part, in the third person. [This book is set in a cemetery in early twentieth-century London and follows the fortunes of two families who have graves side by side there and who get to know each other. In its published form it is told in the voices of the wives, husbands, lovers, children, servants and a gravedigger's son.] When I read it after the first draft I felt it was terrible: boring, like a lead balloon. So I cracked it open and completely rewrote it using all these different first-person perspectives. That worked fine and only took six months, although I rewrote about 90 per cent of it. It is very important for the structure and style to follow and feed on what you are trying to say – form following function.

I also wrote the first chapter of *The Lady and the Unicorn* in the third person and it didn't work, for me, anyway. I feel the third person is a much more complicated issue. In some ways, I have set that as my goal: as the sign of my maturing as a writer. You have the writer, and the third-person narrator, and what is happening; and how much space there is between those things is something that a writer who is in control of what she is doing can play with.

So I need to decide early on if the narrator telling the story about William Blake comes directly from me, or am I creating a narrator who is telling the story? It is very hard to do, and I don't feel like I am really going to be a true writer until I crack that one. I realize that for some writers it may be the other way round, and they say they find third person easy, and that they could never sound convincing inside the head of a Dutch maid! We all have our own strengths, but I am trying to broaden mine.

There have been plenty of people who have said that *The Lady and the Unicorn* [about the making of a set of medieval tapestries] is too much like *Girl With a Pearl Earring*, or that it uses several different voices, like *Falling Angels*. I feel they are probably right to a degree, but it is not deliberate, and I resent it when people say, 'You've found your formula, so you are sticking to it, just so that you will sell a lot of books.' Then I think, 'Oh, for God's sake, if I were driven by money, I would never have become a writer!' I tend to write about what I have been obsessed with in the past or am interested in now, and I have always loved those tapestries. It is not as though after *Girl With a Pearl Earring* I cast my eye around thinking, 'What artwork shall I write about next?' It doesn't work that way. But I am aware of all these things and so I am trying to break new ground with Blake. It is not about a specific artwork, and he is so complicated that it cannot possibly be about one thing.

So I hope to vary my technique, but physically, my method does not really alter. I have a small room at the back of the house where I write, and sit on a chair with pieces of paper, leaning on whatever hardback book is lying around. It is all very primitive. I don't like lines on the paper; it has to be blank, although it can be just scrap paper. I usually have an old manuscript that I am writing on the back of with a pen. If I have to, I can write at the library, but I prefer the atmosphere of my own room. I never write on a bus, or in a café, or anything like that; it just doesn't work.

I always write longhand. I find there is much more connection with words if I touch them somehow. The pen is much closer to the page than pushing a button that makes a letter appear on a screen, which seems very disconnected from *me*. Also, I write more slowly than I type, and I think I write at the speed my mind thinks up the sentence. If I am typing a sentence, I tend to think it faster, and write more sloppily. Then in the editing process, if you have written it longhand, and you start making changes on the page, you can see the changes you've made. And half the time, when I change something, say, moving a section around, I will change it back to where it was again, or move it to a third place. But all traces of editing disappear on a computer, it just *looks* good all the time, and I think that typeset look on the screen is very seductive. I think I am much harder on myself when I see the messy handwriting.

Drafting has changed a lot since the times when someone like George Eliot would write a novel all the way through and then write another draft of the whole book. What I do is a compromise with the computer. At the end of the day I type in what I have written in longhand, and as I type, I change. Then the next morning I will look over what I typed in the day before, and I might make changes then, so I am constantly tinkering with it. But to write a whole draft, and then go back and rework it depends on the book – with *The Lady and the Unicorn* there were four drafts: two before I let anybody see it, and then two edits. But even that was not complete change. From first to second draft is the biggest change, and then there may be quite a big change when you show it to somebody, but after that it is more tinkering.

I never give a manuscript to my husband to read. He is the most important person, so I want him to read it when it is at its best. So he reads it after it has been edited. I don't want him to help me, in the same way that I don't think couples should teach each other to drive! My agent is the person who reads the manuscript first. *Girl With a Pearl Earring* was hardly redrafted at all: that book came out of me kind of like magic. I wrote it very quickly because

I was pregnant, and I finished the book two weeks before I had my son, so I didn't really have time to redraft. And I knew that while I was writing: I made certain aesthetic decisions because of that. I decided it was going to be very simple, short, first person, told from one point of view with no structural experimentation, linear and grounded in the everyday. I sort of had a model of what I wanted to do from looking at Vermeer's painting, so it was following his path, rather than trying to strike out on my own in some different way.

Now I usually write when my son is at school and tend to write better in the morning: I get tired by the afternoon. I try to write 1,000 words on a writing day – which is about three or four pages. It is just enough to get into a scene without finishing it. I think it is very important that you spend more than one day on a scene because you have a different perspective the next day and you can mull it over at night a bit. I keep being a mother and a writer quite separate, but it is difficult, because it will be 3.15 and I will be sitting at my desk, and will think, 'Oh, God, I just need an hour more!' But I can't. I have to go and get Jacob, and at times I find that very frustrating. But I think it also gives me some perspective, so I don't get completely lost. My son brings me back into the world.

But as well as juggling motherhood and writing, I also have the other part of my writer's life, which is doing interviews and going on trips and all that takes up a lot of time. So I have to say 'No' more and more to things. If I said 'Yes' to everything, that is all I would ever do; I would never get a book written. And every time I say 'Yes' to something I have to find a babysitter or find a place for Jacob to be, and there is a lot of working out schedules, which I find difficult and tiring.

For the most part I do all the research for my books myself, although I finally broke down about eight months ago and got an assistant. Actually she helped me with the latter stages of *The Lady and the Unicorn* before she became my assistant. She checked little things at the end that I hadn't managed to find out. I still do over 90 per cent of the research, but just today, she has gone off to get some maps of late eighteenth-century Lambeth and we are trying to pinpoint a year. She does a lot of the foot-work, but she can't read *for* me. She can find the stuff that I need to read, and the map, but it will be me that pores over it with a magnifying glass. She is the foot-soldier and I am the general! Even then it took me a long time to let go of the control of the research. I take notes on so much stuff that I will never use, but only I can see the stuff that will go into the book and what details I am interested in.

I find the mixture of fact and fiction in my books stimulating because the truth is always stranger. I was reading about a circus man who lived next door to William Blake in Lambeth, and I can't not write about him because he was a really flamboyant character, and I am sure he and Blake crossed paths. Then in the British Library yesterday, I read that this man was once bet that he couldn't float all the way down the Thames from Westminster Bridge to where Blackfriars Bridge would be. He was a big man, and he lay on his back, floating, holding two flags upright, chuckling to himself all the way, and won his bet! I thought this was such a fantastic detail that I must include it. I couldn't think up something as good as that.

Sometimes I use facts a bit as a cheat, because if I weave them in with fiction, it will make the reader trust me, and believe the fictional parts of it. So with Vermeer, a lot of the structure of where he lived, whom he lived with, how many children he had, what their names were – all that scaffolding of his life is genuine. But all the things about his character and what he was like, I have had to suppose, or create from what I see in the paintings and what I made up. I think people were willing to go along with that because they felt the rightness of the factual stuff. It is probably much braver to make up somebody com-pletely, but actually, I am not sure that writers ever do. You could say that science-fiction writers make up whole worlds, but it is very difficult for it not to resemble our own world in some way.

We all use reality around us, and for me, it is simply that I happen to go back in time, so, for instance, in *Falling Angels*, Emmeline Pankhurst makes a couple of appearances. Maybe that is a cheat, and I should have made up a suffragette, but I couldn't make up the whole suffragette movement, so it is a balancing act between using fact and more fictional gaps. In *Girl With a Pearl Earring* we do not know who the model for the painting was. Her clothes are plain compared to other women in Vermeer's pictures, but the pearl is luxurious. To me it seemed that the earring was not hers, and I made up that she was a servant called Griet.

I was relieved when I saw the film, because it could so easily have been awful. The only thing I could do at the start was to choose people who I thought understood the book and would remain true to it, but after that I had to let go. I watched the process over the three years it took, and there were moments when it did almost go off the rails, because of the way films are financed. They inevitably have to have an American financer so that they can get an American distribution deal, and any time large amounts of money are involved, the people giving the money want to have some say. So you would get the Americans saying, 'We want to have a bigger name.' And there were big names interested, but then they dropped out, and they got the right cast and the right director. I think it looks beautiful and Scarlett [Johansson] is lovely in it, and you come away with a similar feeling to reading the book, even though of course they changed some things.

Several people have asked what I thought about the film and it is one of the things I discuss on my website. Nobody has any control over that website except me and my sister – I have deliberately kept my publishers out of it. It is not a place where I sell books or am commercial, but is a place where people who are interested in the books can get questions answered and explore a bit more. I am not very good at marketing myself, and feel that honesty is the easiest way, so for instance I do not mind admitting that I might do some things differently in *The Virgin Blue* now.

Having some success has made me more confident in my writing, in that I know while I am writing that people are going to read it, and that is a very nice feeling. Not knowing if anyone will be interested, or even if a book will get published, can be very frustrating, although there is also something wonderful about it. Then you are really writing for yourself and you don't have the pressure of time and expectation from the publisher and from the reader. But if I had a choice, obviously I would rather be the way I am now.

Because I know that I am writing something which will be read by others, I don't want to make it deliberately difficult or obscure, but I don't have an ideal reader in mind. I remember on the UEA course, when we read each other's stuff and then discussed it in class, I once pointed something out in someone's work, saying, 'I don't quite understand what you are getting at here.' And he said, 'Well that is your problem, not mine.' And I thought, 'Oh boy, if you don't think the reader matters, that is not going to wash!' I don't think he has ever been published, so there you go. I feel that kind of attitude is so arrogant, although I do not think you have to spoon-feed people, and I am very careful not to manipulate the reader. I don't want to tell you what to feel and lead you by the hand, but I also don't think you should be left out in the wilderness trying to grope your way around. But I like to leave a lot of gaps for readers to fill in, and in that way it is the reader's book as much as mine. It is a collaborative process.

I am glad that I was able to write a novel about a painting that is not prescriptive. The book is open-ended enough that people love the story, but they also feel they can look at the painting and get something more out of it. I haven't completed the story of that painting. A lot of people, especially young people, tell me that they now look at art in a new way, and I think that is great, because it extends the life of the book way beyond the book itself. It is fantastic, because I have taught them something, but not in a pedantic way. I didn't set out to teach, but inadvertently I have done.

And I, too, love learning about different periods of time and have things come alive that I hadn't really found interesting before. Like now, I am writing about Blake and am suddenly absolutely fascinated by the French Revolution, in a way that I never was before. It makes the past, which can either seem vast and scary, or dull, old and dusty, still very relevant to us. I feel my place in the world is more secure, because I understand better how I fit into it. It is a kind of existentialism in the end, and I think that is what I get out of writing.

# Julia Donaldson

*It is partly due to perseverance that Julia Donaldson's multi prize-winning and best-selling picturebook,* The Gruffalo, *ever got published. First it was so difficult to write that she nearly abandoned it, and then it lay in the offices of Methuen for a year, before it was published by Macmillan. There is now a gruffalo jigsaw, Big Book and soft toy. A play, based on the book, has shown on Broadway and throughout the UK. The book has sold over a million copies, has been translated into 31 languages, and hundreds of children know the words by heart.*

*Julia Donaldson was born in north London, studied Drama and French at Bristol University, and now lives in Glasgow. She started her career as a busker, then wrote songs for children's television, before one of her songs, 'A Squash and a Squeeze', was made into a book in 1993. Her publisher at that time, Methuen, suggested Axel Scheffler as illustrator. Since then, Donaldson has worked with Scheffler a great deal, five books winning awards. But she also works with other illustrators, for example recently, Joel Stewart and Anna Currey.*

*What is less well known is that Donaldson is the author of over 70 books for children; as well as picturebooks, there are novels, plays and educational books. She works from a mixture of traditional tales and her own stories, but most of her picturebooks are written in rhyming verse, and one of her books for older children* (The Giants and the Joneses, *for which Warner Brothers have bought the film rights) includes a made-up language. Julia also writes songs and musicals, and spends much of her time in schools, libraries and theatres, acting out scenes from her books and singing, with the help of her audience.*

**Selected Bibliography**

Children's Books

*A Squash and a Squeeze* (1993), *The Gruffalo* (1999), *Room on the Broom* (2001), *The Smartest Giant in Town* (2002), *The Magic Paintbrush* (2003), *The Snail and the Whale* (2003), *Princess Mirror-Belle* (2003), *The Giants and the Joneses* (2004), *The Gruffalo's Child* (2004), *Rosie's Hat* (2005), *Charlie Cook's Favourite Book* (2005)

Plays

*All Aboard* (1995), *Books and Crooks* (1998), *The Head in the Sand: A Roman Play* (2003), *Bombs and Blackberries: A World War Two Play* (2004)

The following passage is from *The Gruffalo*. With illustrations, it occupies the fifth to seventh pages of a 24-page story, which is about a quick-thinking mouse who comes face to face with a fox, an owl, a snake and a hungry gruffalo:

> On went the mouse through the deep dark wood.
> An owl saw the mouse and the mouse looked good.
> *'Where are you going to, little brown mouse?*
> *Come and have tea in my treetop house.'*
> 'It's frightfully nice of you, Owl, but no –
> I'm going to have tea with a gruffalo.'
>
> *'A gruffalo? What's a gruffalo?'*
> 'A gruffalo! Why, didn't you know?'
>
> 'He has knobbly knees, and turned-out-toes,
> And a poisonous wart at the end of his nose.'

*'Where are you meeting him?'*
'Here, by this stream,
And his favourite food is owl ice cream.'

*'Owl ice cream? Toowhit toowhoo!*
*Goodbye, little mouse,' and away Owl flew.*

'Silly old Owl! Doesn't he know,
There's no such thing as a gruffalo?'

\*       \*       \*

I have a theory that many people end up doing what they wanted to do when they were about six years old. For instance, I have a friend who is a costume designer, who loved cutting out dolls' clothes. In my own case, my father gave me a book of quite old-fashioned rhyming poems, called *The Book of a Thousand Poems*, when I was five. I loved them, and went round reciting them. I also loved 'Listen with Mother' on the radio, which had nursery rhymes and poems, and my granny used to read me Edward Lear poems, so I was quite exposed to songs and verse. My family was also very musical: my father played the cello, and my mother sung in a choir.

So when I was five, my ambition was to be a poet. When people asked what I wanted to be, that is what I would say! Maybe a poet now sounds a rather grand thing to say I am, but I am writing in verse for children, so it is not so removed from what I imagined at that age. I remember my childhood very vividly, and haven't rejected that part of myself. However, later on, for most of the time that I was at school, I wanted to be an actress. I was quite academic, and ended up going to university studying drama and French. As part of the course we went to Paris for four months, and I had just learnt to play the guitar, and used to go busking in the Champs-Elysées. We could only play about three chords, so we sung 'Greensleeves' and 'Plaisirs d'Amore' and things like that. Then a great friend of ours, Malcolm, who became my husband, came out and he knew all the Beatles songs and all the songs from *Hair*, and had a great repertoire that we all performed together.

When we came back to England we got asked to perform at after-dinner cabarets, and for a children's street festival, and a dentists' do, and I started writing songs to order, for the events. We also went on busking, and went to Italy, where I wrote a song in Italian about pasta, and that all led to a career, if you can call it that, in writing songs for children's television. I was still fairly freshly out of university, and I sent a tape to a Play School BBC team, and then they would ask me to write songs on a particular theme. It wasn't even as grand as being commissioned; I think if they hadn't liked a song, they wouldn't have taken it.

One time they sent me lots of postcards from a museum in Belfast, because they were going to do an outside broadcast from there, and I had to write a song about how *amazing* this museum was, based on a postcard of a stuffed polar bear, an extinct fish and a vintage car. I also wrote a couple of musicals around this time, and staged them with a semi-professional company. Then I had children, and as they got older I would go into their school, and help with the reading, and write short sketches for the children to perform, because I found it was a good way to bring their reading on. But then it all just fell into my lap, really! I got a phone call from a publisher who knew one of my songs, 'A Squash and a Squeeze'. It had been on a BBC tape about 10 or 15 years before, but this woman remembered it, and was now looking for picturebook texts, and thought it would work, and that is how my first book, *A Squash and a Squeeze* got published.

After that I got out a lot of plays and things that I had written and kept in a drawer, and sent them to an educational publisher. So actually, I had 17 books, such as readers for schools, published before *The Gruffalo*. In fact educational publishers [who sell directly to schools] have all the best writers, but trade publishers, who sell to shops, are quite snooty about educational books. Mine were mainly for a creative strand of a reading scheme. For instance, I was asked to write some plays based on traditional tales. I had to research the tales, and in fact I found one that I decided to keep up my sleeve, because I thought it could be the seed of a picturebook. It ended up as *The Gruffalo*! But at that time I was writing retellings of folk tales. Sometimes a limitation on vocabulary was imposed, but then there are restrictions when you write trade books too, because if, for instance, it is a picture-book, you have got to have 32 pages.

Anyway, whilst I was doing the educational books, I was really keen to get a second trade book published and sent off several manuscripts, which got rejected. I had several picture-book and younger fiction ideas, which all got very nicely and gently turned down. Most of those I have now reworked, and they have been published in some form or another! The success of *The Gruffalo* has made a big difference, but I would hope that if I wrote something lousy, someone wouldn't just accept it because I was the author of *The Gruffalo*. Editors can be welcome protectors against one's own worst judgement.

When I wrote *The Gruffalo*, I didn't know that Axel Scheffler would be illustrating it, although I had loved his illustrations for *A Squash and a Squeeze* and I did sort of have him in mind. The publisher chose him for *A Squash and a Squeeze*. Publishers usually choose an illustrator who they think will suit your words best. (They do usually ask me first if I like the illustrator's work.) When you see the final result, it is a bit like when you go on holiday: before you go, you've got a picture of what the holiday will be like, and the scenery, and beach, and hotel room, or what-ever, and when you get there it is different, and the pictures in your mind get obliterated. It is like that really with illustrations.

Actually, *The Gruffalo* had quite a long time between me writing it and it getting into print. It had a year sitting on the desk of the publisher who did *A Squash and a Squeeze* because they were going through the throes of being taken over and things, which I didn't know about. I got fed up and very bravely sent the text directly to Axel, because he hadn't been mentioned by the publisher. It turned out that he was now working for an entirely different publisher. Axel gave it to them, and they immediately snapped it up. Then the publication was still delayed for various reasons, like Axel was doing another book.

During that time, I used it a lot in schools. I got children to draw the gruffalo, from my description, and I have still got loads of their pictures. I suppose most of them are a bit more alien looking: more brightly coloured and weird than the furry creature you could plausibly get roaming around in a forest. Axel's gruffalo is more natural looking, but I suppose I had imagined the gruffalo a bit more weird. But I knew straight away what would work. He did several sketches, and one was too much like an ogre, another too much like a wild boar on all fours. But from the start, he got the mixture of scary but stupid just right. That was the most important thing, and he got that just as I had imagined it.

Also, things that now seem obvious, like when I wrote, 'He has knobbly knees, and turned-out-toes,/And a poisonous wart at the end of his nose', it raised the question of how that would be illustrated. Now there are three vignettes throughout the first half of the book, illustrating just the parts of the gruffalo described, so you don't see the whole gruffalo till the middle of the book, but that could have been done with thought bubbles, or there could have been three possible different ways the gruffalo might look.

Publishers tend to see the picturebooks that are illustrated by Axel almost like a brand, their product, where Axel and I are not separated. So even when there is an audiotape of a book, it says it is by both of us, which is a little odd, but is nothing that I would ever argue with Axel about. I don't write a brief for the illustrator, and we work independently, unless it is something where there is any possibility of misunderstanding the text. For instance, in *The Gruffalo*, the third time the mouse says, 'There's no such thing as a gruffal . . . Oh!' I had to make it clear that 'Oh' would be a squeal of terror, so I might add a note, 'page turn here, when the mouse is confronted with real live gruffalo'.

Now, when I am writing a book, it is usually an 'Axel book' or a 'non-Axel book'. For my latest, *Charlie Cook's Favourite Book*, which is a book within a book, within a book, I had, perhaps rather grandiosely, imagined having 12 different illustrators – I hadn't seen that at all as an Axel book, but he has ended up doing that one. But then there will be another one, which isn't his cup of tea, and someone else will do it. My books are fairly different, for instance I have written plays for reluctant-reader teenagers, but I suppose the rhyming stories remain my favourites. I feel that is my own specialty and area of expertise: there are so many good novelists out there.

I think *The Snail and the Whale* is perhaps my most poetic book. I like the way it has got a kind of Jumblies, Edward Lear feel to it as well as the similarities to *This is the House that Jack Built*. I often write within the tradition of stories where the hero wins through against impossible odds, or fairy stories, where it is not the prince who is heir to the throne, but the smallest little tinker. I am very interested in scale and perspective, and one of my favourite children's books was *The Borrowers*. I *loved* the fact that a chess piece would be a statue for the borrowers, or a postage stamp would be a portrait on the wall – that aspect comes into *The Giant and the Joneses*, and also the end of *The Gruffalo's Child*, with the shadow.

That book is also completely role-reversal. It is a joke on *The Gruffalo*, really. There are the same characters, plus the gruffalo's child, and their roles are all reversed, so that the predators who were tricked become the tricksters; the mouse who was the little adventurer becomes the scary monster.

I knew that Macmillan would love a sequel, but children's publishers are so nice, and respectful of one's integrity, that

I wasn't pressurized at all. I had always said that the great strength of *The Gruffalo* was its clever story line, and I certainly wouldn't want to have another *Tom and Jerry*-type sequel, or some soppy thing about the mouse and the gruffalo becoming buddies and learning to count together.

Then what happened was a couple of years before I wrote it, my editor *did* say to me, she was wondering what the gruffalo would think of the mouse. If the gruffalo thought the mouse was this amazingly powerful, clever creature, the gruffalo might have a problem, and go to the mouse for help. I didn't follow that line, but it did give me the idea of thinking what *would* the gruffalo think of the mouse, which gave me the big bad mouse idea. It took ages for that idea to come along, and I wasn't prepared to do it unless I did get a really strong idea.

I can get inspiration from lots of things. I got the idea for *The Giants and the Joneses* because one of my children was an avid collector, and there is a theme running through that book of collecting. *Princess Mirror-Belle* came about because another one of my children had an imaginary friend, who was actually just his reflection in the mirror, but he imagined this friend came out of the mirror. *The Jungle House*, an early-reader book, which has just come out, is from a childhood memory of my own. I don't find the idea the difficult part at all, and I think lots of writers would agree. It is one thing saying, 'I'm going to write a book about an imaginary friend who comes out of the mirror!' What is really, really hard, is what is going to happen: what will be the middle, the beginning and the end?

For me, the plotting is by far the most difficult part. I know some authors do just start to write and it all comes, but I think an awful lot start to write, and they think they are writing a good book, and it is actually unsatisfying, because it hasn't been very well planned. With a picturebook, I definitely have the whole plot in my head before I start, and now I have learned to apply that to longer books as well. I am not saying you don't change it at all, but you have a framework, or map, or skeleton. I do a lot of the work before writing a book, in my head – in the bath, or walking along. Quite often I will go to the library to write, because when I am at home I get distracted. I can write with any old pen, in any old notebook, and do lots of doodling, and try out lots of different rhymes and alternatives. With a picturebook, every couplet is an agonizing process.

With a longer book, because I am quite a quick typist and it is so easy now on the computer, I am afraid I use it. But I find the creative process and the critical process get very intertwined. I have this idealized notion that it would be lovely just to write and write, uncritically, when the muse takes you, even if it is a load of rubbish, and then as a totally separate process, pick holes in it and change it. But actually, I don't do that, and I think the computer makes that impossible, because it is so easy to change things as you go along. I would also like to be one of those writers who has a strict schedule, but for me it is very much all or nothing. When I have an idea or a commission, I am doing it almost night and day, and I bore everyone about it. We might be on a country walk, and I talk about it to my husband and children, or I will be in a daydream in the shops thinking about it.

It can take months or years for the germination of a book. But from the time I said 'Right, I am definitely going to write this picturebook that has been in my mind for so long', writing *The Gruffalo* probably took two weeks, with all the rewriting. I would be at it all day, although not necessarily with a pen in my hand the whole time, sometimes it is better to just do it in your mind.

Because I am quite a prolific writer, I am also very busy with all the attendant things. I am always getting illustration roughs, contracts, proofs, requests from charities, fan mail, author visits – and although it is rather demanding, I quite enjoy all that, because it is displacement activity. So is performing, which also takes a lot of my time. I consider myself a children's writer and a performer, and for me, the performing side of it is equally important. I don't just see it as a way of publicizing my books, but I love acting and singing, and so does Malcolm, so I spend quite a lot of time getting the props sorted, and booking the theatre and actually doing the shows. I think I have been very lucky with the Tall Stories production of *The Gruffalo*. They used my text as a framework for the play and then elaborated within that. I wouldn't have liked it if they had taken my characters and done a different story. I also love the physical nature of that type of theatre, with all the mime and movement.

I don't have an audience for my books in mind. I feel I am very much writing for myself. I am a perfectionist, and I want to write something that I am really happy with. Even if kids couldn't care if you rhyme bananas with pyjamas, or mine and time, I probably wouldn't be satisfied with the imperfect rhyme of the 'n' and the 'm'. I also like to have a nice shape to a line, and so on. But although I am writing for myself, at the same time it is sometimes frustrating that I know I can't use a particular word, because I just know it would be too grown up for children. So it is much harder than, say, writing adult songs.

I don't really know why I do it. There is excitement when you get an idea, although when I am actually writing, it often seems very grinding and uninspired, especially writing a long prose book, which I find really hard. But I think often the things that are the hardest read the best. I *love* the polishing and improving, and I love gloating when I have finished! I think creative people sometimes don't recognize their own creativity, because for them it is normal. My husband would say I am a born writer, and of course I have got to do it, and I have been writing in one way or another ever since he has known me.

I tend to be a bit disparaging of *The Gruffalo*, because it is as if you have got a family, and one of your children is famous and recognized, and you want the others to be too. The seed of *The Gruffalo* was sown, as I said, when I was doing research. That story was about a little girl who goes into a forest, and straight away she meets a tiger, and then tricks the tiger by telling him she is the Queen of the forest, and then all the animals run away, actually from the tiger, but the tiger thinks they are running away from the little girl. I thought I would do a book about a mouse and a tiger. Then I thought it would be nice to have specific predators; I would set up a new dimension if the mouse had already tricked them by pretending he was going to have lunch with the tiger.

So I had my plot, but I couldn't get any good couplet, like 'Silly old fox! You ought to know, you really should, / There aren't any tigers in this wood.' Something like that just didn't seem very strong. So then I thought if the mouse were going to meet some made-up creature, it would be much easier for *me* to write about it. I have just looked at my notes, and see that at first I thought the creature could be a 'snargle' or 'stroog' or 'tiglophant' (I must have been thinking at one stage of having it a cross between a tiger and an elephant). Then I finally thought of the lines, 'Silly old fox! Doesn't he know, / There's no such thing as a gruffalo?' I thought the word had to have three syllables, and end in 'o', and would sound fierce with 'gr' at the beginning, so gruffalo came.

Next, I had to have the mouse scaring the creatures with his description of the gruffalo, so what was the gruffalo like? I wrote down things like horns, ears, claws, legs, tail, and all the body parts of any creature, and then adjectives, like furry, sharp, scary, fiery, and saw what rhymed with what. So I had various alternatives at first for what the gruffalo looked like, and to begin with these were not separated out from the story the way they are now. For example, originally, instead of 'He has terrible tusks, and terrible claws, / And terrible teeth in his terrible jaws' I had 'His face is covered in chicken pox, / And his favourite food is roasted fox.' Or, 'Long sharp teeth and big fat lips, / And his favourite food is fox and chips.'

So I had been going to say that the mouse describes the gruffalo, ending up with his favourite food is . . . the predator.

Then my youngest son said he thought the predators were all incredibly stupid, because just because the mouse says the gruffalo's favourite food is them, they wouldn't immediately flee. They would think the mouse was on his *way* to meet the gruffalo, and they would have time to eat him first. So that is why I had to add the bit, 'Where are you meeting him?' / *'Here,'* which makes it all imminent, as though the gruffalo could be coming any second. That meant it had to be very condensed, and I had to have a couplet which just said something like, 'Where are you meeting him?' / 'Here, by these rocks' / 'And his favourite food is . . .' And that made it really hard, having some food rhyming with rock, or log, or whatever.

For example, when the mouse sees the snake, he says he is meeting the gruffalo by the lake, 'And his favourite food is scrambled snake.' When the mouse sees the fox, he says he is meeting the gruffalo by the rocks, 'And his favourite food is roasted fox.' But when I came to write the piece I have quoted with the owl, there wasn't something which rhymed with it. I couldn't say, 'Where are you meeting him?', 'Down by the fowl, trowel, or whatever, and his favourite food is something owl,' so I had to turn it around, and write that he was meeting him, 'Here, by this stream / And his favourite food is owl ice cream.' I had to write lots of different foods down, and lots of different forest settings, until I got something that rhymed and fitted in.

I enjoyed doing it up to a certain point, and then the second half was terribly difficult, and I nearly gave up halfway through the book. *A Squash and a Squeeze* had been published by the trade, but I had other things rejected, and I had very little confidence, and thought, 'They're not going to want this one!' Also at that time, the fashion for picturebooks was much more, 'I love you little one; will you always love me?' and that sort of thing, or, 'If you smile, you'll find you've got lots of friends; you just didn't see them before!' and a rather wordy book about a monster just didn't seem to be the right thing.

The part when the mouse goes back, with the gruffalo following him, threatened to be incredibly, tiresomely long-winded. Something like, 'They went a bit further, and then they came to the place where they had seen the fox, and they looked around, and sure enough there was the fox, and the fox saw the gruffalo' and it could have gone on for pages and pages. But then my middle son said, 'I really like this, Mum, you must finish it!' Then I just hit on 'They walked and walked till the Gruffalo said / I hear a hiss in the leaves ahead.' And that was a really nice concise way of getting over the problem. It is so difficult, but important, to make it concise, and for every word to count.

I remember being told stories as a child, and, you may think this surprising, *hating* total repetition. I couldn't stand stories that went, 'He went further and met a hen, and he said to the hen, "Are you my mummy?" and the hen said, "No. Have you seen the pig?" so he went further and he met a pig.' And they go on and on exactly the same. That is why, although there is a repetitive structure in my books, what I think is nice, is when the child knows there is going to be the same pattern, but they don't know *how* the gruffalo would cook the snake. And in the bit quoted the mouse says, 'It's frightfully nice of you, Owl, but no', whereas he also says, 'It's wonderfully good of you, Snake, but no', so there is a little variety. Children love a chorus that repeats, and joining in the bit they are prepared for, but I don't like the whole thing to be like that.

A lovely thing about my job is that it is not just solitary; you meet lots of nice people, and lots of children. And now my husband of 31 years, who is a doctor, is going to take a sabbatical year off, so he will come with me and do shows and work in theatres, so it is a bit like back to our busking days. Except that now we tend to sell out theatres in advance! The shows are usually an hour long, and we tend to do songs, and dramatizations of the books. We use the audience a lot. So, for instance, if we are doing *The Magic Paintbrush*, Malcolm is usually the emperor, but we will get a dad to be the wise old man on the rock, and we give him a cloak. And we choose five children to be the 'baddies' with Malcolm, and I choose various villagers to be with me, and the whole audience recites the villagers' lines from a flip-chart. Malcolm also does the giant in *The Smartest Giant in Town*, where he has to do a striptease, although he has fairly voluminous spotty boxer shorts and a string vest!

For me, nothing can quite equal the thrill of *The Gruffalo* being accepted, because although it wasn't my first book, it was my first trade book that I had recently written. And although there is nothing wrong with educational books at all, there is something special, even just in the eyes of the world, about having a book that you know people are going to be able to go into a bookshop and buy. When I got that letter from Macmillan about *The Gruffalo*, I am sure I leapt higher round the room than I have leapt before or since. I leapt round when it won the Smarties Prize too, and even though my life is very fulfilling now, nothing quite equals that heightened pleasure of the early days.

# Margaret Drabble

*Margaret Drabble was born in Sheffield in 1939 and educated at Newnham College, Cambridge. Graduating with a double first, she joined the Royal Shakespeare Company at Stratford, married actor Clive Smith, and understudied for Vanessa Redgrave, before writing her first novel at 24. Drabble comes from a family of writers: her father was a barrister and novelist, and her sister is the author A. S. Byatt. Her second husband is the biographer Michael Holroyd.*

*Margaret Drabble's books are valued for their elegant psychological analysis and subtle humour. She has written 17 novels as well as short stories and non-fiction. She has been compared to Austen and Dickens, won many prizes, and was awarded the CBE in 1980, yet surprisingly, she still feels uncertainty about her writing.*

## Selected Bibliography

Novels
*A Summer Bird Cage* (1963), *The Millstone* (1966), *The Ice Age* (1977), *The Radiant Way* (1987), *The Witch of Exmoor* (1997), *The Peppered Moth* (2001), *The Red Queen* (2004)

Biographies
*Arnold Bennett* (1974), *Angus Wilson* (1995)

Editor
*The Oxford Companion to English Literature* (1985, 2000)

The final sentences of *The Needle's Eye*: Rose, the protagonist, is looking around Alexandra Palace. In contrast to the hand-carved lions that adorn Rose's parental home, the lions here, near where she has chosen to live, are mass-produced:

> But it was a toothless lion, any boy could draw on it. She peered at it, closely. It was grey, it looked as though it were made of grey brawn – small specks and lumps of whiteness stood out in the darker background, diamond-shaped flecks. She wondered what it was that it was made of – cement, concrete, plaster. And the Palace itself. What a mess, what a terrible mess. She looked back at it. It was comic, dreadful, grotesque. A fun palace of yellow brick. She liked it. She liked it very much. She liked the lion. She lay her hand on it. It was gritty and cold, a beast of the people. Mass-produced it had been, but it had weathered into identity. And this, she hoped, for every human soul.

\*        \*        \*

I chose this piece because it seems to me to represent my middle style, when I was writing realistically, but using symbolism, and writing with a lot of social optimism and social commitment. It is about London, and hope, and aspiration: so it brings together a lot of my feelings about London life, domestic life and social life in one image. It is also quite interesting that that part of the city hasn't changed very much – some of London has become transformed since I described it in the 70s and 80s.

Since I wrote that, I feel the world has changed, and I have noticed that in my later novels a different tone has come in, which is less optimistic, harder-edged, snappier and more bad-tempered, perhaps. This is just the interaction of me and the world, and a sense of having to express oneself in a different format. I don't know whether it is also that the realistic novel no longer seems such a viable medium for connecting with people.

One of the great social changes of the past 20 years is that we now live in a multi-cultural world where the recognizable social realism of the nineteenth century has been exploded into fragments. It is very hard now to write in a deeply rooted British tradition. We used to call it the English tradition, but now the word 'English' itself, has turned into 'British', and the word 'British' has turned into 'global', so we are writing in a very different context. I think I first noticed this happening to me acutely with my novel *The Witch of Exmoor*, which is a sort of political fable rather than a realistic novel, although it looks like one. It was written towards the end of Mrs Thatcher's Tory ascendancy, and Britain just wasn't the same place that it had been.

That novel has a young, black, Guyanese, aspiring politician in it: very much a New Labour man. I found it difficult to write, so that when I came to *The Red Queen*, my most recent novel [where an eighteenth-century Korean crown princess, or her ghost, tells her story, and chooses a modern-day British scholar as her envoy], I liberated myself from time and space. I tried to write from a much more removed perspective altogether, and ask what is it that we essentially are, when we are not bound by culture, politics, or society. What is left after all that is gone?

I wrote *The Red Queen* having read the crown princess's memoirs, and being completely gripped and bowled over by them. I wondered how it was that this story from so long ago was having such a powerful effect on me. Then I constructed a contemporary life in Babs, which had some resonance with the crown princess's life. Babs's life is not at all like mine: I have never lost a child, and although I am very interested in medical ethics, I am not involved with it. But I did think that there was *some* reason why a long-ago woman's story was reverberating with me, and I think it is to do with female experience being beyond time.

I worked very hard on that novel, trying to make the Korean background authentic, without making it a historical novel, but I was also haunted while I was writing it by an encounter with an adopted Chinese child, which is an incident that occurs in the second half of the book. I met a child who had been adopted by some people I know, and I did have the experience of being absolutely transfixed by her gaze. And I thought, 'What is taking place here, between two people who know nothing of each other, and whose lives have no common thread, but who are staring very hard at each other, as though there is something to say?' So that is very far from social realism; in fact it is completely cross-cultural, and I found it fascinating that at my age such interchanges happen.

Actually I have just been invited back to South Korea for a couple of weeks. They are publishing my book in Korean, and I am quite nervous because I know that it is considered problematic as cultural appropriation. They are all being very nice about it at the moment, but I can't really tell what is going on between the lines. That book was as though this woman had seized me from outside and said, 'Look, there is all this happening in the world that you know nothing about!', which was very interesting for me. More usually the books come from themes that I have been brooding on for a long time, in my own life as it connects with the world.

In *The Red Queen* I don't think the crown princess is *me* at all, but she is asking many of the questions that I ask. So I have a narrative voice that has an agenda of enquiry. There is a strong, even controlling, narrative voice in most of my novels, but it is not necessarily mine. In *The Radiant Way* I tried to split the narrative voice between three strong female characters, which actually I think worked quite well, and it is not at all clear which of them I identify with most closely.

In fact I would place myself almost precisely halfway between Liz and Alix, and not at all like Esther, who is an aesthete and an academic and a pure scholar. Half of me wants to be smart and trendy and showy with big parties, like Liz; and half of me wants to be a social worker, and I feel caught between those two attitudes and styles of life. But I suppose most deeply I identify with Alix, because I was brought up with the social conscience and the desire to think you are doing good, even when you are not. That goes very deep into me and my family background.

Most of my strongest characters are women. I don't think I am writing *for* women, although I know I have a larger female readership, but then more women read novels than men anyway. I feel slightly more comfortable writing about women, but that doesn't mean that I think it is good that I feel comfortable. I have to work less hard. I worked very hard in *The Needle's Eye* with Simon, and also in *The Ice Age*, trying to get into the mind of a businessman. I am writing a novel at the moment in which the narrative is split between a male and a female character.

I know that when I read a novel by, say, Martin Amis, or Justin Cartwright, I realize that men, in their novels, think a lot about sex, in a way that I as a woman can't describe. So when I am writing from a male point of view, I am missing out a lot of what they would have been thinking about. I am aware of that. I don't think that means my characters are completely unconvincing, because they can think about business, or their children, or their jobs, or God, or the absence of God: but I cannot write about male sexuality from a male point of view, which means I have to work harder to make all the other bits convincing.

I do use personal experience in my writing: I think every writer does, and if they say they don't, then they are not telling the whole truth. I use things I have seen with my eyes, people I have met, and experiences I have had, but I also invent. So there is a degree of closeness to my experience that is very variable. Sometimes I take people in my books into places that I have never been to, and to experiences that I could never have had. On the other hand, in my first book, *A Summer Bird Cage*, I wrote a novel about sisters, and of course, I have a sister. I thought I would write it so it would end happily, and everybody would be friends, and then I would never need to write about that again – a rather naïve concept of the underlying plot, but that was my plot.

I have to say I don't read my sister's work. I did read *Possession* with great admiration, but I haven't wanted to read her later work, and I know she hasn't read mine. There is a difficulty, because we use the same material and have been to the same childhood places. I don't want to read her version of my child-hood place, and she doesn't want to read mine, so we just ignore each other, which is uncomfortable, but understandable. My father's work, I enjoyed very much, and indeed helped him with it, in that we talked about it. My husband and I talk a lot about books, but we never interfere with each other's work while it is in progress. I have found him extremely supportive, poor chap. He has to put up with my moods, and I have to put up with his, which are often work-related. But that is more to do with the rhythm of living with somebody, than the actual interchange of work.

I started writing as soon as I left university. I used to write little bits and pieces at school, but then at Cambridge I was too busy doing other things. But when I left, and married my first husband, who was an actor, I was alone a lot of the time, as I think young wives quite often are, to their astonishment, and I filled in the time by writing. And before I knew where I was, that's what I really wanted to do. It happened by a combination of accidental circumstances, though you could say they weren't accidental, in that I had chosen them. But I found myself becom-ing a writer. I also had small children coming along, and it is a good career to combine with that.

I am afraid I found it very easy to get published. The first pub-lisher I sent my book to liked it very much and published it, so I had a false impression of how easy the world is out there. But I think in those days, in the early 60s, publishers were looking for young writers and weren't overwhelmed with manuscripts.

I mean all credit to my excellent editor for taking a chance on me, but there were young women coming up, and it was a good, new market.

Although I have written many books, I do not find it easy. It comes fairly easily when it is going well, and I have little patches of two- or three-day bursts when it is good. But then doubt and anxiety and all sorts of difficulties creep in and I get very worried. I find it harder to write now. I think that as you get older the facility disappears: you question yourself more, and wonder why you are doing it. When I was young I just wrote for my life, as it were. Now I find it harder to justify what I am doing.

In some ways, when I was young, I thought the world was a piece of cake, although actually I was also a very neurotic, depressed person, and always have been. I am kind of two people at once all the time. I am this person who thinks everything is easy and I can just stride forward and it will work, and I am the person who is completely collapsed and imploded and thinks that nothing will work. So I am up and down. Some days I feel I have been very successful and it is a boost to my confidence, and I can always say to myself, 'Well, you wrote those books, and there they are!' Other days I feel they are all a failure; they were never what I meant to write. I think this is very much a writer's temperament: we oscillate between feeling 'What a genius I was when I wrote that', to 'How on earth did I get that published? Was it publishable?' There is that feeling of uncertainty that I have every day of my life.

I think I write partly from habit, and because it is something that involves me more closely than anything else that I do. I feel completely involved when I am writing. I don't notice the passage of time, whereas I do when I am doing almost anything else: I've got my eye on the watch, or I am wondering what's going to happen next. When I am writing I become absorbed, and, intermittently, euphoric, and I think, 'Yes, that's really good!' Or, 'Yes, that has solved that problem!' Then you are riding on a wave, and suddenly it all unfolds ahead of you and is going in the right direction. But that is very rare, and most of the time it is a struggle.

The way I start writing has varied over the years, but I usually start with a theme. The early books are about the conflict between being a mother, and trying to have a job, and trying to be a person, and justifying your education. It is a theme of how to be all these things at once. *The Ice Age* was very much a money novel: it was all to do with the oil crisis and the failure of England, and all the characters arose to illustrate the condition of England. Similarly, in *The Radiant Way*, the characters were chosen to represent money and the extraordinary Thatcher revolution, and the way people's lives were changed as a result of that. So those books were thematic. *The Peppered Moth* came from a desire to lay my mother's ghost to rest, and that is my most personal novel, which is closest to my personal memoirs. *The Red Queen* just came and hit me from outside like a bolt from the blue. I had no intention of writing it at all.

I don't like repeating myself, or the feeling that I am going into a format mode. I felt comfortable with *The Seven Sisters*, because I had gone into an old linear mode, and I did that because I was so exhausted by *The Peppered Moth*, which was a great challenge to me on many levels. Then I got bored with the linear mode, which I had used in my very early novels. The novel I am writing at present has a science background, which I wanted to see if I could do. There is a feeling that I want to extend and find new voices and places to be, otherwise I get tired with myself. I am fascinated by Anita Brookner, for example: she writes the same novel so brilliantly and beautifully, but it is the same plot. And I think how reassuring it would be to be able to do that, but something in me won't let me go back. I have to be going forward, even when I am going nowhere.

I can't write when I think I am going to be interrupted, so I tend to go to our house in Somerset, on my own, to write. Then

I don't have to worry about meals or anything. I used to write best in the evenings, but I am better in the mornings now. For me, it is good to get up, have a cup of coffee, listen to the news, and then start work. I find it hard to work in the evenings, or if somebody's about to ring up, or if I am about to go shopping. I can't work when I have got a shopping list on my mind. If I could have back all the hours that I have been writing shopping lists while trying to work, I would be as prolific as Dickens!

I now work on a computer, although I didn't at first. The first novel I wrote on the computer was *The Seven Sisters*, in which the narrator has quite a close relationship with her computer! I think you can tell that she is using the computer all the time, as was I. But the novel I am writing at the moment has got in a terrible mess, because you discover you can do all these tricks, like find words, and go back, and weave in, and it is like a terrible coral reef that has built up. So I have no idea what the narrative flow is, because it has been building up incrementally in weird orders. I think that is the danger of writing with the computer.

I have very rarely known quite what the ending of a novel would be when I started. I usually have a sense of direction and a sense of the mood of the ending, but I have never quite known how the eventual plot will work out. I do more and more rewriting, because of the computer. It is so annoying, knowing that you can go back and rewrite and insert! Now I find I insert twice over, because I have had the same brilliant thought in the middle of the night and put it in, and then realize I put it in last week. I find that really annoying. But I think it is to do with getting older. I think when you are young, you write with a much more powerful narrative drive, and now I toy around more, and then you have to spend time unpicking, as well as putting it together.

I heard Kazuo Ishiguro talking about Martin Amis, and Ishiguro said, 'I can't write those big, bold, colourful, literary sentences: my style is restrained.' And that is true, and I thought it was interesting, because my own style jumps around terribly from literary, to informal, to banal. I don't like reading a book where the level is sustained too high: I get tired and feel I want a rest now! While I am writing, I sometimes think an image, or words, come to me that are definitely literary, in that the words themselves make the meaning. And I think, 'Oh, that is a bit of a literary novel.' But then something in me tells me I have got to go back to something more pedestrian that will let the reader breathe, and relate, and catch up. So I think my style wanders between the literary and the middle-brow and the positively banal in a very curious way.

I also write non-fiction, which uses a completely different part of the brain. In a way, it is very hard work, but it is much less high-risk. You don't feel you are going to win or lose it all with what you are doing. You do it honourably and well. You may not be able to do it perfectly, but you can do it well by working harder, whereas with a novel you never have that sense of security. I am not in the first rank of biographers, because I don't address the formal problems in the way that serious biographers do.

I am glad I have kept going and have had stamina and been a hard worker. I was trained by my parents to do that. I am proud of having made so many contacts through books, beyond the people I know personally. I feel I have touched people, and interacted with people that I could never physically or geographically have known in my life. I find that very rewarding, and feel I have been adding towards some world view that is in constant flux and change. I feel that I have been part of that process through what I write. Even if the books are completely forgotten, there will be things that have changed, and I have been part of that change.

At the moment I am trying to finish a novel which I think is completely ghastly, having had a year or two of struggle with it. I am at the stage where I think, 'I'll get to the end, but who knows if it is publishable or not?' That is what I usually feel, though actually, all the books I have finished have got published. But with every one of them I think, 'This will be the one that will be turned down.' And that day will come. Because supposing I go on writing till I am 92, that one will be turned down! In fact, I felt that even when I was 30. I felt, 'I'm sure they are not going to like this one.' The insecurity of the writer's position is extreme. I tend to think it is just me, and I am paranoid, but in fact I know a lot of writers have exactly the same anxieties.

I have very many ideas, but I don't have the faith in them that would deserve two years' commitment to execute, so lots of little ideas wither without taking root. I really admire the stamina of novelists. The stamina of someone like Henry James was just phenomenal. It used to take me about a year and a half to write a book, but they have got quite a bit longer, so it is now around two years. And you take risks, and you know that your editor or publisher will say, '*Why* did you do that?' And you say, 'Well, I thought I'd take a risk.' And they say, 'Well, we just wish you hadn't'. They don't actually say that, but you imagine they are going to!

I have had a pattern of doing two or three novels and then a non-fiction, so I feel perhaps I should do that. I don't want to do a biography, because it is very, very hard work, and I don't want to invest five years, at my age, on something that isn't necessarily going to be a great work. So I am not quite sure what I want to do next. I want to get to the end of this novel. Michael says to me, 'Why don't you do something else altogether?' But of course you become what you are.

# U. A. Fanthorpe

*U. A. Fanthorpe famously started writing poetry late in life, after a career as Head of English at Cheltenham Ladies College. When she left, she worked as a hospital receptionist in Bristol, and it was this experience that led to her first collection of poetry in 1978. Born in 1929, Fanthorpe became a full-time writer in 1989, and is now very prolific. Some of her most successful poems are in monologue, such as her brilliant 'Not My Best Side', which looks at Ucello's painting of St George and the Dragon from the viewpoints of the damsel, the dragon and the knight. Many of her poems are questioning, and display compassion for ordinary people, an interest in history, and England at a time of change.*

*Fanthorpe's list of awards is awesome. She has had numerous fellowships, and holds honorary doctorates from the Universities of West England and Gloucestershire. She was the first woman to be nominated for the post of Oxford Professor of Poetry, and was a leading contender for the post of Poet Laureate in 1999. In 2001 she was made CBE for services to poetry, and in 2003 was awarded the Queen's Gold Medal for Poetry.*

*All Fanthorpe's books are dedicated to her partner, Rosie. If you write to Fanthorpe, you are likely to get a reply from Rosie Bailey, pp U. A. Fanthorpe. They are inseparable. Rosie was present throughout the interview, and occasionally U. A. would defer to Rosie for confirmation of what she was saying. Both are charming, polite and endearing. Although Bailey is herself a poet, at readings she supports Fanthorpe, and together they perform a double-act of Fanthorpe's work. Dressed in matching black men's suits and cravats, their readings are unforgettable: moving and entertaining, with the slightly formidable-looking Rosie putting on accents and adding delightful wit and humour.*

**Selected Bibliography**

Poetry
*Side Effects* (1978), *Standing To* (1982), *Safe as Houses* (1995), *Consequences* (2000), *Queuing for the Sun* (2003), *Collected Poems* (2004)

This poem is the ninth in a sequence called *Consequences* from a book of the same name. As I asked for about 15 lines, U. A. Fanthorpe chose to omit the fourth stanza, but the poem works surprisingly well without it:

ASK A SILLY QUESTION

'The age of chivalry is gone. That of sophisters, economists and calculators has succeeded.' (Burke, *Reflections on the Revolution in France*)

King Dick or King Harry? Theme park or business centre?
Choose, England.

I choose peace; I never get it.
Takeovers and overtakers, de-militarised zones,
Kings dead in ditches, displaced persons,
Class war, sex war, civil war, war. Tortures,
And other irregularities.
                    Somewhere, all the time,
A dog is finding something beastly to eat
Under a hawthorn. Does it matter
Who it is, Harry or Dick?
What matters is that people live
The ordinary all-in-a-day's-work life of peace. . . .

This was the battlefield. Birds, hedges, sheep,
And long November shadows. *Hedge laying*
*On Saturday. Strong clothes, please,*
*And bring a packed lunch. Remember,*
*This is a haven for wildlife, with a variety*
*Of wild flowers and different species*
*Of butterflies. Please do not pick or harm.*

Far off, the inveterate voice of battle:

> *Who's 'im, Bill?*
> *– A stranger.*
> *'Eave 'alf a brick at 'im.*

This is all there is.
No Andes, no Outback. There's no more than this,
And the sea chews away at Suffolk.

*      *      *

This poem covers quite a lot of the things that are important to me: looking after England and the people, which is the theme of the whole sequence of poems. This one has got the different voices of England. I always think of the first voice as the Vicar's wife, who is slightly bossy, but well meaning; and then the old *Punch* joke, 'Who's 'im? And the national response, "Eave 'alf a brick at 'im.'

I nearly always write in free verse. It started that way when I worked as a receptionist in a mental hospital, and the first thing I wanted to write about was the patients. I tried writing about them in verse and sonnets and things, but it came out too glossy and too simplified, really. It seemed obvious that I needed to cut things up and be abrupt and use the patients' own words as much as I could.

The reason I went to work in the hospital goes back a long way. When I was at Oxford as an undergraduate, I had an accident – my foot was crushed, and I had to keep it up in the hospital. I got to like the nurses and the patients and the ward maids and everyone who was around there, and I distressed my parents a lot by saying, 'This is what I want to do. I want to work in a hospital!' Of course I didn't, I did what was the usual thing in those days, I went and taught.

But I never really felt that I was as good a teacher as everybody else. I could always hear 'laughter in the next room', as Osbert Sitwell says. I didn't feel I was right for it, but took a long time to disentangle myself, which is why I didn't really start as a writer until I got away. Teaching is a very creative thing to do, and you put all the creative side of yourself into it. There wasn't any creative energy left until I got away. Then I didn't think of being a poet: I wanted to write a novel, and make money, as one does.

My sister-in-law's children had just all gone to school, and she joined a thing called Manpower, which found jobs for you. I thought I could do that too, and I had various jobs in Bristol: one was a telephone clerk at Hoover, and one was working in a petrol company. Then I gradually felt I could do better than just having temporary jobs, so I applied for a job in a hospital, thinking, 'I know what hospitals are like.' Big error. The hospital I had been in was a general hospital, but the one I applied for was a neurological hospital, where people were quite disturbingly odd and strange, and that is what provoked me into writing.

I decided to call myself U. A., rather than Ursula, from experience in the early days at school. When a new teacher would come in and ask my name, and I would say, 'Ursula Fanthorpe' I knew she would get it wrong, and say 'What?', and I would have to say it all over again. It is an over-the-top sort of name. I mean, your name is admirable: a sort of straightforward name.

I wrote quite a lot because I felt I had got to make up for the time lost. I rather grieved that I had missed out writing about being a young person, and that I was firmly middle-aged when

I started. Actually I don't like writing about myself, really. I was brought up not to use 'I' in letters, and one of the ways to avoid that is to write in the persona of somebody else. It is also much easier, because you can think how they would say things.

This may sound strange, but the thing that usually comes first when I am writing is truth: to get it straight, to get it right. And that is something that the poem, while I write it, will teach *me*. If there is something that is not quite genuine, or put in only for laughs, I will try to cut it out. Also, being a poet, I try to cut out as much as possible, really, to leave the reader all the work to do. I don't start writing until I have got a line or two in my head. Sitting with a bare piece of paper in front of me is a terrifying thought, but I don't do that; I wait till I have a bit in my mind and then a bit more will attach itself. I always think of the first thing I write as being the first line, but sometimes it turns out to be the last line – I have misidentified it: you have to be versatile and adjustable.

I haven't mastered the computer. This [Rosie] is the computer expert, who gets it all down for me afterwards. I write on paper. In the hospital, I used to write on the back of old admission sheets: I use anything that is not too daunting, even the back of my hand. In the same way, I don't have a study where I work; I just do things on the dining-room table. I don't want to frighten the muse away! I like it to look as unofficial as possible. I can write anywhere: it is *easier* going uphill, for some reason. I go for walks with the dog, uphill, and it is a lovely situation for a poem to start, or to be continued. There is usually a notebook or the odd bit of paper in my pocket.

I revise infinitely. That is one of the jolly things, I think – when you have got it basically there, and you just have to tinker. I love the tinkering process: I could go on forever. When they're published I would still like to tinker with them and alter them again. One poem I wrote took four years, but another I wrote overnight. A good time to write is when I wake up very early in the morning and my thoughts are kind of muddled between now and the night with dreams, and I get some quite interesting insights then. Once or twice I have just sat up in bed at about 5 am and written a poem, but it doesn't happen very often.

One of the most important things is trying to get the words right. English is so rich in words: there are so many possibilities of meaning that I have to go on endlessly trying one word or phrase after another. I also try to be very economical in the use of the iambic pentameter. It is a great help in making a funny point, because there is a slight pompousness about it, but I mustn't do it too much, or people will notice. Alliteration is also important to me. I did language and literature at Oxford, and that meant studying Anglo-Saxon. I was swept away by Anglo-Saxon poetry, and am still, even if I read it in translation, which I mostly do these days. It is marvellous poetry, and is at the roots of the language, and alliteration is very strong. I find myself writing alliteration without even trying. I think it was Tennyson who said he had to go through and cut out a lot of his alliteration.

I am not a methodical writer, like a novelist, where you have got the real dedication of so many words a day. I usually have several poems going on at the same time. If it is a good idea – sometimes it is, and sometimes it isn't – I get a kind of adrenalin feeling that it is going to be fun and exciting, and I want to get on with it straight away. Other times, as at the moment, I have been asked to write a poem about Fanny Burney, the eighteenth-century novelist, and I know I haven't got to do it for four months, so I am taking my time and thinking about it a lot. That is a different sort of process, without the excitement, but with the pleasure. It is nice to be writing.

It happens quite often that I am asked to write something in particular. For instance, if I am asked to go to a reading, they might ask me to write a poem about the place. Or the other day, I went to a school, and was asked to write one about Palm

Sunday. Mostly, I think, 'Oh, I couldn't possibly do that! It doesn't interest me.' But then I find that it links with something else in my mind, and I can do it. I could never have put all the hard work into being Poet Laureate that Andrew Motion does. I admire him immensely for all that he has done. He is always on the radio, or organizing competitions, or something. I feel worried for him in a way, because he may not have time to write his own stuff now, and I always feel that writing your own stuff should come first.

I now enjoy readings. I didn't at first, because I had a lot to learn: it is not an easy thing. The first one I did in London, I read completely black, sombre poems, and I could see the audience getting more and more depressed, but I didn't know enough to fling in something to wake them up and make them feel happy. Now I try to end with an upbeat one. I like people to laugh at what I have thought: it is a nice feeling of reciprocation. I use some classical references in my work, which at the start my publisher, Harry Chambers, was dead against. So for a while, I tried very hard not to bring in any classical references of any sort. Then my mother died, and for some reason I was swamped with feelings that came over clearer in the Roman mythology, with people like Virgil, and I couldn't keep it out. So my publisher gave up on me after that, and instead said he didn't want any footnotes. Now he allows me those.

My mother was a remarkable woman. You never think that at the time: everybody else's mother is much nicer – more maternal and motherly. Mine was a fighter, and absolutely splendid during the war, which is where she sort of belonged, really. I was conscious that she had given up a lot so that we could exist. She had had a splendid job in the civil service, but they sacked you in those days as soon as you had children. So I was always trying to make up to mother, by doing well, things that she had missed out on. She appreciated that: her ambitions for my brother and me were very great – I'm not sure we always came up to the mark.

At the moment I just want to achieve my next poem, called 'The Duration'. I am mulling it over all the time. It is about being young and vulnerable, when people don't tell you the whole truth, as people don't in wartime. I keep doing bits of it and then something else crops up. I write best either when I am at home, or we used to have a narrow boat and that was a lovely place to write on because there was no post, no phone, just water and moorhens. But although I am doing other things, like washing up, the poem is there at the back of my mind. [Rosie chips in: 'I would say, you are really writing all the time, in a way.'] You need to take all the opportunities when they occur; a thing I am rather bad at.

Where we live now, in Wotton, in Gloucestershire, the people think of me as a poet, and say, 'Oh, she's the poet!' But I don't think of myself at all like that really, do I? [she asks Rosie, who replies: 'No. Poet is a sort of grand word that you wouldn't ever apply to yourself. And it is a bit of a conversation stopper to say you are a poet!'] I think people think poets are a bit strange, and should be dead by 28 of consumption! I don't write for an audience, or for myself, but for the poem, really. I am writing for Rosie, in a way, because she is the critic, and will run her eye over it and tell me where I have got it wrong. But I don't think about her at the time when I am actually writing it, only afterwards. [Rosie: 'I see the poems first, but at quite a late stage in their writing.'] Similarly, I don't like the poem to be typed, or put onto the computer, until I am really sure of it, because if it is too soon, the whole thing goes dead on me, and may get discarded altogether.

It is great living with another poet. She knows what I am on about! [Rosie: 'I wouldn't consider myself a poet, really.' U. A.: 'Oh, I would! She has just had her first volume published and people are very thrilled with it. They speak of her directness . . . No, she won't let me talk about it.' Rosie: 'No, but I do know that I can relate to U. A., because we have worked at poetry in one way or another for the last 30 years. So we talk the same language, and that is helpful.' U. A.: 'It is, it is.'] Sometimes naïve friends at home imply that I have special insights and special responsibilities. Of course I don't. My thing, if it is anything, is to be a human being. I am working at that.

# Julian Fellowes

*Julian Fellowes is an actor and Oscar-winning screenwriter whose self-assured public image belies a masked sensitivity. Born in Egypt in 1949, he grew up in England, and attended Ampleforth College, then Cambridge and then drama school. He has appeared in supporting roles in more than 40 films and TV shows. While in rep he resided in damp digs during the week, but he was invited to house parties in stately homes where his laundry was done at weekends. In some ways he lived a double life – and this was to prove very useful as his writing career developed.*

*Starting with romantic novels (two under the pseudonym Rebecca Grenville), Fellowes turned to writing for the BBC where he adapted* Little Lord Fauntleroy *and* The Prince and the Pauper. *He remains especially celebrated for his adaptations of novels for the small and large screen. But it was his script for* Gosford Park, *his first original screenplay to be produced, which won him the Oscar. A spate of acclaimed work followed: social satire, clashes of class loyalty, moral dilemma as well as wry humour are Julian Fellowes's forte.*

*When he agreed to be interviewed, Julian wrote to me on a card bearing an engraved picture of a large country estate – Stafford House, the Dorset home he shares with his wife, Emma Kitchener. Emma is a descendant of Lord Kitchener and lady-in-waiting to Princess Michael of Kent. Julian, himself a descendant of a Rear Admiral who served with Nelson, proposed to her 20 minutes after they first met. At the time he was 40 and she 25. They married within a year and it was Emma who encouraged his writing. Now Julian Fellowes packs theatres at literary festivals. While signing books for people in long queues, he half-rises to each lady in polite salutation.*

**Select Bibliography**

Screenplays
*Gosford Park* (2001), *Vanity Fair* (2004), *Piccadilly Jim* (2004), *Separate Lies* (2005)

Plays
*Mary Poppins* (2004)

TV
*Little Lord Fauntleroy* (1995), *The Prince and the Pauper* (1996), *A Most Mysterious Murder* (2004 and 2005)

Novels
*Snobs* (2004)

The following is from a scene about halfway through the screenplay of *Separate Lies*, an adaptation of Nigel Balchin's *A Way Through the Wood*, which Fellowes wrote and directed – Emily Watson and Tom Wilkinson play the roles:

INT. VICARAGE DRAWING-ROOM. NIGHT.

ANNE
Bill's going racing at Longchamps on Saturday. He's leaving tomorrow and he's asked me to go with him.

JAMES
Right.

ANNE
He thought we might stay on in Paris for a couple of weeks.

JAMES
I see. So have we reached what they call 'the end of the road'?
Do you want a divorce?

ANNE
I just want everyone to stop being so unhappy.

*This does not look like being fulfilled. JAMES laughs.*

ANNE
What is it?

JAMES
Only that I'm in Paris next week as you very well know.

ANNE
No, I don't.

JAMES
For the grand, final meeting on Whirlwind?

ANNE
I'd forgotten. I'm sorry.

JAMES
Don't be. Please. It'll be fun. You with your lover, me slaving
in misery across the way. My work's always been a source of
hilarity for you and I'd like to think you can still get a good
laugh out of it.

ANNE
Please don't be like this.

JAMES
Why? How should I be? You can have suicidal, bitter or glad-to-be-rid-of-you except I can't manage the last one so I think I'll stick with bitter.

ANNE
Will I see you? When we're there?

JAMES
Fuck off.

ANNE
I suppose you'll be in the George Cinq.

JAMES
Fuck off.

*Looking at him slouched in his chair, his face doughy with misery, his hair untidy and damp with sweat, she would very much like to embrace him if she could do so without retracting anything. But she can't. So she goes.*

\*       \*       \*

*Separate Lies* is about a man who thinks he is very happily married and that his life is fabulous, and it isn't, which he can't see because he is very bound up in himself. His journey in the film is coming to understand that he is not in control of everything and that he has to let go. This moment comes when he already knows his wife has a lover and he has started to address that, but now she is actually leaving him, which he didn't realize. I always like scenes when what they say and what they are feeling are two completely different things, and that is really what I write.

I think that on the whole, when people are very educated, and most of my characters come from a fairly educated background, they use words to protect themselves. They use words to create veils to stop their feelings making fools of themselves, but you can see through it. I think that scene is quite a good example of a man who is in *horrible* pain, but his instinct to make a joke, and retreat behind the joke, is not quite suppressed, until he gets to the point where he just tells her to fuck off, because he can't go on hiding what agony he is in for another minute. The film is based on the book by Nigel Balchin and is one of those stories where you make one bad choice and one lie multiplies, so that suddenly there are 100 lies and you can't go back to before the first lie.

When I very first started writing I just wanted to have something published. I wrote some 'bodice-rippers' when I was about 19 and published two of them under women's names and all of them under false names, because I knew that they were nothing to do with *me*: there was nothing in them that I was saying. It was like a game where I wanted to find out if I could publish them. But after three, I decided I didn't want to be that kind of writer always. And I think I was aware at 20 that I didn't have anything to say, really. So then I stopped writing except for the occasional magazine article.

Then years later, in the early 80s, I was living in Hollywood, and people used to give me scripts to read, and say, 'I've been offered this by Paramount, what do you think?' And I would read it and I'd say, 'Well, it is all right up to page 37, but then you don't believe that the doctor would come back', or whatever. I started being an unofficial script doctor, and looking back, I think that was a very important part of it all. Then I co-produced, with John Davies of London Weekend television, a Piers Paul Read novel called *A Married Man*. It was scripted by Derek Marlow and I worked as a kind of script editor on it, constantly returning to the book, which drove him mad. So by that time I was really thinking in terms of script.

When I went to drama school, in the 70s, everything was about the theatre. But the one thing that going to Hollywood reminded me of was my love of film. It wasn't a great success career-wise: I didn't become a star. I came back because the high point was second choice to replace the dwarf on *Fantasy Island*. But it took me back to the camera. When I was on stage, I was quite interested in the rehearsal, and getting the performance, and when I was on stage doing it, but not the rest. Whereas when I was on a film set I was checking how the lighting was done, and interested in sound, and how the make-up worked: all of that I was gripped by. I realized that the camera has a dimension of documentary reality which intrigues and involves me.

But when the curtain goes up and there is that sofa and two chairs and someone comes on talking very loudly, the unreality of the stage is a bar to me. I think if I were living in the nineteenth century I wouldn't find that. In fact one of the most interesting theatrical experiences I had was when I went to see *The Woman in Black* and I was really scared. I suddenly thought, 'This is what the theatre was for the Victorians. It wasn't an acceptance of its unreality and an essentially intellectual exercise, it was jumping because you were given a fright.' But they didn't have film as a comparison. Now, this is the film generation, and for me, if I have a day off, I go to the movies.

Anyway, in the 80s, my acting career was not delivering what I wanted from it. I am not complaining, because I always kept working, but I wanted to be on the A-Team and it wasn't happening. So I thought I ought to have a plan B, and I thought that would be producing. I sold an idea to the BBC, and they suggested a writer, and I did a lot of work on those scripts, even though, again, I didn't get the credit. But because of that, the head of the department gave me the job of writing a new adaptation of *Little Lord Fauntleroy*, and that was when I really officially became a writer. I wasn't fixing anything; I was making a new adaptation of a book. There was a lot of prejudice against making it then, because the subject was unfashionable, and they said no one would watch it, but it *was* made and I think it got the largest viewing figures they had ever had for the 6 o'clock slot. It also won an Emmy in New York and did incredibly well.

Ironically, because I had stopped concentrating on acting so much, it started to do much better. It is rather like when you adopt a baby you get pregnant. But now my writing career had started too. I think the acting helped the script writing. Actors understand dialogue, and it doesn't actually matter whether they are good or bad actors. They always have something worth listening to to say about dialogue, and if you don't listen, you are stupid. Some of their comments will be, 'I haven't got enough to say.' But as long as it isn't that, if they say, 'This speech ought to be broken up; this thought isn't right; there is one too many words in this', I would say they are right 90 per cent of the time.

I can say that recently, when I was directing my own script, I was very interested when the actor said 'I want to cut this', and so on. Although you may not always agree with their solution, you can see their problem, and you come up with another solution. I think that unlike novelists who take to screenplay writing, which can be difficult, an actor has a natural idea of what is 'sayable'. One is never supposed to say anything in one's own favour, but I *would* say this: when I first started writing scripts, I do think I had an instinct for what is sayable. For instance, one of the things you often see with novelists is that every page has got a speech for about two-thirds of the page. In *Gosford Park*, my first feature that got made, there is one speech in it, with Helen Mirren talking about being a perfect servant. But by that time the audience has invested so much in her and the situation, and they realize of course that she is the murderess, so they are ready for a speech. But you must never over-use that. No screenplay should have more than two at the most, preferably one, and quite often none.

The reason I got to write the script for *Gosford Park* was pure chance. One of the scripts I had written before was an adaptation of *The Eustace Diamonds* [Anthony Trollope] for an actor/would-be producer, called Bob Balaban. He knew Robert Altman, and was trying to set up a project with him. Altman likes to take a form, like a Western, or a thriller, and not quite make that, but turn it on its head. And he thought he would do the same with the country-house murder-mystery. He would use it as a vehicle for an examination of that way of life. But as he got into it, he realized that he needed someone who knew how that life worked, and the basic logistics of running one of those houses, and he couldn't find a writer who knew that.

Then Bob Balaban remembered me, because he had got to know me a bit before. I had always been the kind of person at the edge of the upper classes, who gets to accompany debutantes because he is safe in taxis. I was a sort of analytical member of a class system that had been unfashionable in dramatized fiction for 30 years. So I had rarity value. I was an insider and yet an observer in many houses like Gosford Park, and they were usually interesting. For instance, I remember a friend of mine was once invited to a house party in France, which she felt might not be particularly entertaining. She decided to go, but to take all of her dirty washing with her, and her sewing and mending, so that at least something would be achieved if there was not much else to do.

She put all her dirty washing in an old pillowcase, but realized her mistake on arrival when a servant took her luggage and whisked it away. Desperately she made an excuse to go to her room. Everything was neatly unpacked, but there was no sign of the old pillowcase. At the end of the weekend her suitcase was packed for her: all the dirty linen, beautifully clean, was packed in tissue paper. On departure the maid said to her, 'I hope you do not mind, Mademoiselle, we took the liberty of putting new elastic in your knickers.' She was mortified. That was the sort of thing that happened.

Anyway, Bob Balaban thought, 'There is nothing to lose', and so he said to Altman, 'Well, there is this guy who probably *does* know all that stuff, but he has never had a script that has been made.' So they rang me up and had a chat, and then I was asked to put down some ideas for characters and storylines. I rushed out and got every Altman video I could find, so I knew it would be a multi-character, multi-arc movie, and I thought of things to fit that.

Then I was asked to write the first draft, and at the end of that I was asked to go out to California to work with Bob Altman. But it *absolutely* wasn't until the end of the first draft that I thought it might happen. Later I learned that Bob Altman felt exactly the same. He didn't have any faith in the idea at all until he got the first draft, and then he thought, 'Oh, I don't know, I think this might work.' So we were both complete unbelievers. But I knew that I had to give it everything I'd got because if it didn't work, and if I was replaced as writer, and someone else wrote it, I'd have to kill myself.

My initial stage of writing was the characters and what was going to happen to them within the film – so in that sense it was narrative. I started with a series of little narratives without knowing how they were going to interlock. In a way it was a dream, because it was the product of many years' thinking about these people. For example, it has always struck me that there are principally three kinds of unhappy marriages for aristocratic women: one is that they marry a man they despise or don't like, because they can live in a certain way if they do; one is they marry their social equal and everyone approves, but they are bored to death; and one is they marry for love and they later come to resent that the husband is not providing them with the way their sisters live. Each one of the sisters in *Gosford* is an example of that. So there were certain mind-games going on, but really they were individual stories, which later got plaited.

When you write a film now, people are committing a lot of money to it, so you have to have a narrative structure and a pretty thorough synopsis before you go to script. I rather ignore the financial aspect whilst writing: I think you should take out the ball and the naval battle later. While I am writing I do tend to cast the parts in my mind, not because I think those actors will play them, but to get a different voice in the characters. Otherwise there is always the danger that all the characters will speak with your own voice. So I might, in my mind, think of them as Clark Gable, or something. What was odd, in *Gosford*, was that four of the characters I thought of, did play the roles.

A film, and a play, as I now know, has a period when there is only the writer and the producer. Then there is the director, then the casting director, and each time your control of the material is diminished, because their input is added. The final stage is the actors, who take the material you have given them, and if they are good, they make it more than, or different from, what it was when you wrote it.

I stayed on set throughout the shooting of *Gosford*. This was not actually for rewrites, but because Bob didn't really realize at first that the class system was a huge minefield of trip wires. On one level, he didn't want to look a fool. But on a deeper level, he thought that if we could get all the details right the film would acquire a kind of patina, even for people who didn't know that a footman doesn't knock on a drawing-room door but does knock on a bedroom door, or whatever. He felt when all these details were put together the film would acquire a substance which normal servant-acting films don't have, and I agree with him 100 per cent.

If you were doing a Brahmin wedding, you would get a Brahmin in, and so Bob got me. The problem was that I was there to stop him making a mistake by accident. But you don't want someone there constantly telling you, 'She wouldn't be in the dining-room; she wouldn't call her that; she wouldn't do that.' So it was *incredibly* annoying for Bob and quite draining for me, because all I ever said for 12 weeks was 'No'. If everything was right, I didn't keep leaning in saying, 'Well done, Bob, what a good choice.'

At the time, I didn't really appreciate the fact that he never said, 'Look, I am a world-famous film director. Who the bloody hell are *you* to keep stopping me doing what I want?' I mean, he did say, 'Oh, fuck off!' But we were just these two men fighting, and I *now* really admire him for that, because I think the temptation to win an argument through status is very great. On the other hand, I think he was right to put up with it, because I think it was a good movie in the end.

Winning the Oscar for it made an enormous difference to me. Suddenly I had an identity in Los Angeles as a film writer. I had adapted *A Way Through the Wood* by Nigel Balchin about a year before. At the ceremony I was sitting near Tom Wilkinson and had already shown him the script. He wanted to do it, but neither he, nor I, added up to a package. But afterwards, he had been nominated for acting, and I had actually won, and I said, 'Do you think this means we might get that going?' Before the Oscars I was trying to sell it as a script, but having won the Oscar, I thought, 'No, damn it, I am going to see if I can *direct* this', which was my ambition. So my agent hawked it around saying, 'There is a catch. If you like this script, it is already written and not very expensive to make, but he wants to direct it.'

And so, what is now called *Separate Lies* got accepted on those terms. Nor was it a commission in the way that *Gosford* had been. It is very rare that you write a script and someone makes it. I know it happened to Sylvester Stallone, and I take my hat off to him. But for most writers, probably what they are writing will serve in their life as an audition piece. And it will be because it is very well written that somebody who wants to make a film about wheelbarrows thinks they may be the one to write it. Normally directors and producers have got 15 projects they want to make; they are not usually looking for a project.

I am still fairly in the first flush of girlhood with all this: there are still roads to cross. Personally, I feel that I have said just about all that I have got to say about class, and I would love to feel that

that was it. I am much more interested in moral choices. All my principal characters are in a moral dilemma where they have to make a decision. It interests me that very few of us have a black hat/white hat morality in our lives, and we are almost always trying to seek a choice that won't offend our morality, but at the same time will hopefully achieve our ends. That seems to me the spike that most of humanity is impaled on.

I am interested in murder, too, in the sense of how normal and fairly decent people can get themselves to a stage of their lives when murder seems a reasonable option, and how that terrible path was trod. I am also very keen to write a contemporary American screenplay, and that is what I am looking for. I am trusted to write anything English, anything period, and even, though it hasn't been made, anything period American. People think of me as this funny old English guy, and in every career there are some barriers you still have to break down. I would also like to do a real thriller date movie instead of an art-house movie.

I think I would be lying if I didn't concede that when an original works there is a kind of pleasure, in that it is completely your baby; you're not a step-parent at all. And that is very thrilling. With an adaptation it is a different discipline, although actually everything is new. One of the things that a lot of people have difficulty accepting with an adaptation is that it has changed. A journalist came up to me after *Vanity Fair*, when we were launching it in Venice and said, 'In the film, when Becky is going to Queen's Crawley, she gives Amelia a present. But in the book, Amelia gives Becky a present.' To which I replied, 'Well, if that is our main problem, I think we are in pretty good shape.'

There is an absolute reluctance to concede that when a TV show becomes a movie, when a book becomes a play, when a film becomes a stage show, it has got to be reborn. That was very much the challenge of *Mary Poppins*. With a big musical, you have got to have a show that appeals to the whole family. You cannot make a children's show that costs what *Mary Poppins* cost, so you must deliver a really enjoyable evening for the adults, which in itself is a different brief. You can make a children's film and the parents will go in, if it is a local cinema and has not cost a great deal, and if they do not enjoy it particularly, it is no big thing for them. But if they have gone to London, booked five seats, stayed in a hotel, organized a dinner – they don't want to do that if they are not going to have a good time.

The great pressure of an adaptation is not to be disappointing. With adapting something like *A Way Through the Wood*, there is a freedom in that nobody knows the book and what I choose to do with the book doesn't matter so much. The easiest is to adapt a book that nobody knows. The next easiest is to adapt a book that everybody knows. The most difficult is to adapt a book that nobody knows, but they all think they know. And that was *Vanity Fair*. Nobody has read *Vanity Fair* since they were at school, but they have a memory of knowing the book, or they think they know it because they have seen it on the BBC.

So I would have critics saying, 'Oh, but in Thackeray's *Vanity Fair* Becky is the villain.' Becky isn't the villain in the book: Thackeray *adores* Becky. The only people who criticize her are the other characters. The author's voice defends her all the way through and in fact he was criticized by his own publisher because the heroine was unacceptable, which is why Thackeray called the book 'a novel without a hero'. It is quite tiring to get criticism that is not really right.

I came on board *Vanity Fair* when Mira Nair [the director] came on board, and I liked the earlier writers, Matthew Faulk and Mark Skeet: we get on extremely well. As I said to them at the time, 'Within five years tops, you will be rewriting a script of mine.' Mira wanted to begin again, not because there was anything wrong with their script, but because she wanted to make it her own film with her own script, and I came on it to work with her.

I think my gift, to be honest, is being able to write realistic dialogue set in the past. There has always got to be one thing that you know how to do. Some screenwriters have an extraordinary grasp of narrative and can structure a thriller so that the audience is literally on the edge of their chair all the way through. I don't know how to do that, and I would have to have help. I would love to be able to do it, but it would be a real challenge. I can structure an emotional story, I can structure a journey, but with a thriller, you are not just creating arcs that interlock, but you are manoeuvring the audience. In certain films, you can feel that being done to you and then you resist it, and the brilliant films are the ones where you are not aware of the manipulation but you are just terrified.

But I think dialogue is my gift anyway, and I do a kind of stylish dialogue that is quite attractive to listen to, but doesn't sound too stagey. I don't really know why, except that I think I talk like it. I talk in complete sentences. And I think that I talk in a slightly period way, even though obviously I am a modern man saying it now. I construct sentences in a way that might be interpreted as slightly old-fashioned, which is why it is easy for me to write period dialogue.

I also think I am rather good at writing women, because I think I am quite feminine. I know I don't look at all feminine: I look like a sort of English lump. But I was the fourth son, and my mother was terrified that we were going to grow up not having normal relations with women, apart from romantic relations. So our house was packed with women all the time, because she was determined that we should have women who were friends who weren't girlfriends. My father also had women who were friends, which for his generation was quite unusual: he would have lunch with women who were absolutely not girlfriends at all. So I grew up with a lot of my best friends being women.

My mother was very strong, and very good-looking. Now there are men who are made nervous by strong women, but I am made nervous by weak women: I don't know what they want of me – the sort of clinging vine type. My wife is very strong and very good-looking. I didn't notice any similarity, and of course, my mother was tiny, and Emma is very tall, but several of my friends commented on how much my wife was like her, and I can see that. There is something about very strong, intelligent, good-looking, rather bossy women that makes me feel safe. So I suppose from that comes a certain admiration for that type. There are usually some very strong women who are proactive plot members in either my screenplays or novels.

My novel *Snobs* is pretty closely drawn from my own life, with people being amalgams and mixtures and so on. Similarly, in *Gosford*, my great-aunt is the start of the Countess of Trentham. Also just little things – when my mother was first married, my father had a very frightening great-aunt who they used to stay with. My mother was a very keen smoker but was far too nervous to smoke downstairs, and so after they had officially gone to bed she used to sneak up the attic stairs and go into the room of the head housemaid with whom she was quite friendly, and they would illegally puff away out of the window and talk: they were about the same age. And this woman's room was covered in pictures of film stars and they would talk about films. And of course, years after the death of my mother, and I am sure the death of the maid, that is Elsie, the head housemaid at Gosford Park.

I think some people felt that it was rather bad form that I was drawing attention to the fact that all this sort of thing was still going on. There is a kind of universal agreement amongst 'toffs' not to garner any unnecessary publicity: they don't like publicity, and now that they are not a political class, they don't need it. Actually I didn't mind their objection, because in a way, I think it *was* rather bad form. I am not saying I am sorry I did it, because I think we all have to write about something we know and which hopefully not everyone else knows. But I could see why it was annoying.

Individually, sometimes people are angry if they are in a book, but more often than not they are pleased, and more often than that, they don't recognize themselves. Sometimes they think they are in it and they are not, but they come up to me and say, 'I think I know who you based so-and-so on.' and of course they are wrong, but you don't like to say so.

I am hoping to do *Snobs* for TV, but there is quite a lot of prejudice against that, rather interestingly. They don't like dealing with the modern upper class. They can deal with period, but with any modern drama, you sense there is a fear amongst the heads of departments that they will lose some kind of status, because they don't get moral points. They are not all like this – I mean Jane Tranter is fab – she'll do anything she thinks might be interesting. But I was surprised, given the fact that it is a bestseller here and in America, and I am this kind of Oscar-winning writer and all that nonsense; I would have thought it was a pretty good package.

As for the physical act of my writing, I do it on a word-processor. I don't always write in the same place, because sometimes I am in the flat in London and sometimes I am on location, and in fact I get more done on location in funny characterless hotels than in my writing-room in Dorset. More important for me is the time. I write better in the morning, and the discipline that I completely fail to observe, but I should, is to use the morning for writing and the afternoon for rubbish, like answering letters and bills and the mechanics of being alive, or for checking stuff I have already written. But I tend to waste too much of the morning on all that.

I go through weeks when I can hardly write anything and others when I am quite busy, but there is a point in every day when you can't go on. And it isn't a very long working day: if you manage to get four hours' solid writing work it is pretty good – normally it is more like one or two. It takes something like three months to write a screenplay. You write most of it in about three weeks and then spend about six weeks fiddling with it. I do a lot of fiddling with the official first draft before everyone else has a chance to fiddle with it. But if I started a contract, and at the end of three months I still didn't have a script to show for it, I would be a bit worried.

But a line might come to you in the middle of the night, or in a traffic jam, so it is very difficult to say *when* you are working, exactly. I suddenly had the idea how to solve one plot problem the other day when I was getting changed to go out to a party. You are sort of infected by a script or a novel while you are writing it: it is in your waking bones. Then when you start shooting logistics come in, like, 'You can't shoot this scene in a ballroom, it has got to be in a bus shelter', and you have to start adjusting the information to fit the demands. That is the job. If the act is ten minutes too long, you can't then go into a sob about every line that is cut, because in the end you are a craftsman in a *business*, as well as an artist lying there with flowers in your hair.

I never, ever put in camera or lighting directions in a script. I think when a director reads it, it is just irritating. I think he thinks, '*I'll* decide if it is a bloody close up, thank you very much.' I do do quite a lot of stage directions in the initial draft, because I think it has to read like a short story. I think you have to create the film in the mind of the reader. Later, when you have sold it, and it is going to be produced, you can eliminate an enormous amount of the directions. But one of the things I think is fatal is the film-school idea of writing the directions in very abrupt shorthand. It is impossible to read and puts off 99 people out of 100, and I cannot imagine why they tell students to do it.

Actually, I enjoy writing novels more than scripts, because I enjoy the process where you are just working with one publisher and it is just your voice. On the other hand, in life, if it seems that you are good at something, then if you don't do it, you are a bit of a dope. I was quite a good actor, but there were quite a lot of people who were better at it than I was. I had an option in another career, where I was able to achieve the level and choice that I wanted. But I do find it all pretty hard work. What I would really like to do is just go for a walk! But I can't go for a walk and have everything else that I want.

Acting is fun while you are actually doing it, but writing gives you satisfaction when it is done. I have just had some wonderful notices about *Separate Lies*, and when you read those, your heart does sing a bit, actually. The four elements of my life are acting, directing, writing screenplays and writing novels, and I suppose I would like to do all of them, but get to the point where I was doing less *work* than I am now, so that I was living more *life*. I started late, and I think I drove away my good luck by being too desperate, rather than ambitious. I created a kind of desperate aura because I wanted it too much, and I wouldn't just let it happen.

I don't think it is coincidental that my whole career improved after I married. My wife is not a writer or actress, but she calmed me down. And because she was very young and very beautiful, she gave me confidence and a sense of status, so that I no longer felt pathetic. It is not surprising that almost immediately, I walked into one of the best acting jobs I had had in years, in a series directed by Danny Boyle, called *For the Greater Good*. From then on, I started to get a much better level of work and the productions I was setting up started to go. Then I had this rather thin time while I was writing scripts for about three years and nothing was getting made, but I was still acting really interesting parts.

I hesitate to sound like a sort of hippy, but I think my aura or karma altered, and there is something about striving for an inner calm, so you are not so manic, that ends by attracting people to you and with people's success. My wife is a bit psychic, although I never know whether I believe in it or not, and she said to me once, 'The success you want will come not from your acting, but from your writing.' Since this was when I was still only doing

*The Prince and the Pauper* for BBC Children's Hour, it wasn't definitely on the cards. There were two groups of people I was working with, both nice, but of the group I was working with least, she said, 'Those are the ones who are the gateway to what you want.' It was for someone in that group that I subsequently wrote *The Eustace Diamonds*, which was the direct gate to *Gosford*. Anyway, she was right.

# Sara Maitland

*Sara Maitland arrived for her interview having just had a morning swim, her long hair still wet. While talking, she tends to chain-smoke and very often has her eyes closed, but her hands are in constant motion. The fingers of one hand might tap the table as though playing an imaginary piano; she wrings her hands and gesticulates in the air.*

*Maitland is a novelist, short-story and non-fiction writer and teaches on the MA course in creative writing at Lancaster University. Her novels range from the Somerset Maugham award-winning* Daughter of Jerusalem, *about love and infertility, to the 'magic realism' of* Brittle Joys, *about glass-blowing, friendship and an angel. Her latest collection of short stories celebrates the menopause and gives new life to old legends. While contemporary 'children's authors' often write of war and death, Maitland writes fairy stories for adults. She also writes non-fiction, on subjects such as religion and feminism, and she is working on a book that explores silence, both historically and personally. In addition she has won prizes for radio plays and worked on a script for Stanley Kubrick.*

*Born in 1950, Sara Maitland came from a large, noisy, happy family. Having lived in London and Scotland, and been married to a vicar, she now lives alone on the moor above Weardale in County Durham.*

## Select Bibliography

Novels
*Daughter of Jerusalem* (1978), *Three Times Table* (1991), *Home Truths* (1993), *Brittle Joys* (1999)

Short Stories
*A Book of Spells* (1987), *Women Fly When Men Aren't Watching* (1993), *On Becoming a Fairy Godmother* (2003)

Non-fiction
*A Big Enough God: A Feminist's Search for a Joyful Theology* (1995),
*Awesome God: Creation, Commitment and Joy* (2002)

These are the final two paragraphs of the story 'Bird Woman
Learns to Fly', which is the last story in the collection *On
Becoming a Fairy Godmother*. A middle-aged woman, with two
broken wrists, has been out for a drive with her son's best friend:

> We are at Dunstanburgh Castle, on top of the cliff, with miles
> of open coastline stretching north and south. Even as we turn
> towards the car and escape from the bright enormous exposed
> spaces it is not clear to either of us if this moment will last long
> enough. We have to walk to the Jaguar. He has to drive some-
> where. My wrists will start aching. We may yet, one or other or
> both of us, see sense. Or what would pass for sense. We may
> turn giddy, vertiginous, lose height, come down. But it hardly
> seems to matter. Now, now his arms hold me and we are flying.
>
> Perhaps we too will be storm-wracked, bone-broken, but I do
> not care, for I am flying now, hard against the wind itself and
> my joyful curiosity still outweighs my fear.

*       *       *

I started writing with a certain commitment to telling the truth,
particularly within feminism, telling the truth to people who
deserved it. I really feel that 1970s feminism survived, because
of, what I would have called then, our gay sisters, and that was
*never* acknowledged. When newspapers wanted to write about
it they would dash round desperately finding someone with
three small children: lesbians were being 'invisible-ized' again.

I was also, later of course, influenced by my husband. He was an Anglo-Catholic of an extreme sort, and most of them, most of the people we hung out with, were gay, actually. It was how it *was*. So I lived a lot with the gay male culture at that point, and kind of loved it. I am a fag-hag.

My main character in *Brittle Joys* is a fag-hag, and I describe one in a story in *Women Fly*. [They have women friends, sometimes husbands, but their closest friends are gay men who confide in them, and who they enjoy looking after if needs arise.] I suppose you write about your friends, and most of my friends, both male and female, are not very heterosexual. I have never identified myself as a lesbian, and don't think that I would choose to, because I am not. I am very interested in ambivalence, and what happens around the fringes of gay culture. Another very big influence was HIV. I wrote a number of kind of benefit stories for that community. Camp is great fun to write.

I write a combination of things that I know, mixed with fantasy, but I feel I know the fantasy too. I think that every eight year old believes that they can fly: they haven't quite found out how to do it yet, but I try to recapture that astonishing sense. I had a very happy childhood and I think that affects one's imagination very deeply. My pre-adolescent childhood was idyllic. I had lots of brothers and sisters, all close in age, with perfectly well-off and deeply loving parents. I think I was able to keep a lot of that sense of power which gets knocked out of children if they are not happy.

When my father died in 1982 we sorted out his desk, and very much to everyone's surprise, we found a drawer in which he had kept things that we had done as children. We found my first novel, which I had written when I was eight! I had immensely laboriously written out the story of one of my teddy bears and its life. I had done it for his birthday one year and had completely forgotten about it. So in that sense, I have always written. But I got a bit diverted in my teens, as one does, and although I wrote a bit of poetry, I *really* started writing when feminism started: the two for me went very closely together, and I am still not 100 per cent sure why. There was something about feminism that gave me stories fresh, and I began writing short stories towards the end of my time as an undergraduate at Oxford, around 1970.

Quite a lot of the stories were retellings of classical mythology with a feminist slant – which is actually what I write now! Although at that time, I didn't see it as a career thing at all. Then a friend of mine at Oxford became a bright young thing in publishing. She was at Duckworth's, but Faber and Faber were doing a series of books, and they asked her if she knew of any short-story writers, particularly women, who might be included in this. She suggested they look at some of my stories and Faber published them in 1973.

When I first started writing fiction I was in a women's writing group, later called The Tales I Tell My Mother Group, which produced a book. It was rather a distinguished group because Zoë Fairbairns, Michèle Roberts, Michelene Wandor and Valerie Miner were all in it. We talked quite a lot about how to represent feminist culture in fiction without it coming over as propaganda. We decided that if one in every 20 people were gay, then a very large number of feminists would be lesbians. So we had this rule that you had to put one into every story! It was a kind of joke we had, which of course we didn't stick to, but which avoided the endless lesbian-coming-out novel – which after all had been perfectly competently written by a large number of people.

My stories tend to be very moralistic. When Angela Carter was still alive, I was complaining to her that a reviewer had compared my short stories to hers, and I said I was fed up with being sub-Angela Carter, and she laughed and said, 'You don't want to worry because we are fundamentally different. I am a 60s libertarian and you are a 70s moralist.' And I think that was a very accurate perception of hers. The term 'magic realism' has been used about my work, but I don't think it quite describes it. Some

African writers have taken up a phrase to describe their writing, which is 'spiritual realism', which is religiously based. I rather like that term, and it is what I would use to describe my writing.

Toni Morrison has defined spiritual realism quite interestingly as being writing where you actually do believe the magic. I think it is fairly clear that in *One Hundred Years of Solitude*, Gabriel García Márquez doesn't actually believe in all his ghosts, and in that sense his book is more Western. But I think that in some African writing, *The Famished Road* being a famous example, at some level Ben Okri believes in the spirit-child, and that Toni Morrison, particularly in *Beloved*, believes it too. I think in a very Western way: I write much more out of that tradition.

There is a writer called Paul Magrs, who has written a string of novels intentionally grounding magic realism in the English working class. He and I came up with a phrase that we both used for a while, which was 'queer realism' – realism which is informed by culture, particularly male gay culture. I think that is rather nice as well. But it is rather hard, as a middle-aged, vicar's wife, to use queer realism to describe your own work, without confusing a lot of people. I got a review of *Women Fly When Men Aren't Watching*, which said it was very muddling writing, because it isn't quite avant-garde, but it is magic realism on the vicarage lawn. And I think that is fabulous! The magic I write is very matter-of-fact: the stories are grounded in a social reality.

I have written some short stories in which the main characters are not women, but almost entirely the central characters are female, and rather like me, and they certainly get older as I get older. Curiously, not all my readers are women. Two people who have written serious, academic, studies of my work have both been men: one gay, one straight. Usually, I do not have a reader in mind. I wrote a radio play for my daughter, who is an actress, and I did write that as a kind of present for her and for her to act in, which she did. It was enormously good fun.

I have done quite a lot for radio: two technical dramas and two series for Holy Week that were somewhere between fiction and theology, which actually, I am very proud of. They are unusual and original and genuinely communicative. During the five-day run up to Easter, the Short-Story Department gave a morning slot to Religious Affairs, who filled it with little talks on pious themes. Then one year the producer decided to do some religious short stories. The first year they did four old ones and commissioned one from me. Whenever people want someone to do something a bit religious they tend to think of me, because there aren't many literary writers who are prepared to countenance religion! I wrote a story that was a kind of monologue by Mary Magdalene.

Next year they asked me to do five monologues of women from the Bible, linked to the theme of each day of Holy Week. So there had to be some Last Supper on Thursday and some Crucifixion on Friday. Two years later they asked me to do some more, and they were the ones I really liked best. They were not biblical, but were a series of stories of a middle-aged housewife's conversations with her guardian angel, and events in her daily life replicating the events of Holy Week. So, for instance, the story of the betrayal by Judas becomes a self-betrayal, where a bloke comes round to get her to sign a petition against having an AIDS hostel in their village, and she has to work out what to do. She betrays her own principles and then unbetrays them. They are quite funny stories and they bring together a lot of my concerns.

A lot of my work is non-fiction; it is theology. But I have also written a book of garden history, and I worked for Stanley Kubrick, although he died before the screenplay was written. He was extraordinary: not just weird, which he was, but he was one of the most intelligent, best-read people that I have ever worked with. He had very clear ideas about what he wanted to do; so working with him was extraordinarily exciting, but also completely unnerving and impossible. The film eventually became *Artificial Intelligence: AI*, which Spielberg took over.

But if such a career existed, I would like to do Radio 4 afternoon stories. I think they are the most wonderful things to write, because they have to be a contained space – you can persuade the reader to read a tiny bit slower or faster, but basically they are 14 minutes. And short stories are my favourite genre.

My idea is normally sparked by a chunk of fact. For example, 'Why I Became a Plumber', which is one of my favourites, about a woman who has a mermaid in her loo, was written because I encountered three quotations using the same term 'the relative silence on flushing' within two weeks! One quotation was from a pamphlet on the menopause from Boots, one was from *Simple Plumbing*, and one was from a guide to birds. As soon as I had read the three, I thought, 'I have got to write a short story about this: there has got to be a way'. So I was literally plotting the story onto those three quotations – think of a plot, in fewer than 3,000 words, in which somebody could be using a plumbing manual, a bird book and a menopause leaflet! Actually, she doesn't literally use them all, but it was as crude as that: when I saw the third quotation, I knew I was going to write a story.

The story 'Bird Woman Learns to Fly', about the woman in love with the teenager, came out of a discussion about HRT. I have a friend who is militantly pro it, and she gave me a photograph of an X-ray of somebody with bad osteoporosis in her wrist, to make me think about it. Anyway it was lying on the table, and my son, who at that stage was a zoology student, came in and said, 'Mummy, why have you got a picture of bird bones?', and I asked what he meant, and he showed me, and the two were just so alike, because birds have hollow bones, to fly. And I thought, 'How wonderful!' and the story came from how alike the bones were.

I chose the closing lines from that story to quote in your book for two reasons. One is because of the last line of all, which is the end of the book, 'my joyful curiosity still outweighs my fear', which I think, at the moment, is as near as I have got to a credo.

For me that is the case: I go on being more interested. I wrote an essay in a Virago collection about the menopause, called *A Certain Age*, in which I say that I am not as frightened as I probably ought to be, because when I was little I had no fillings in my teeth. We were taken to the dentist every six months, all six of us together, and the dentist would say, 'I wish all my patients were like this!' and then we would all go home. So all these kind of horrors have turned out to be more interesting than horrible, and I think that is how my life has been too.

The second reason is that the passage manages to make reference to a good many of my central themes. Flying has always been a constant metaphor in both the novels and the short stories. Actually, the sort of flying we now do is not the flying of fantasy. If you go on an aeroplane, which is a desire people have had for three or four thousand years, it is exactly the opposite experience to the dream: you sit inside, totally passively. But there is something about flying that does represent people's sense of personal freedom. When the book was reviewed, someone said all the images represented sex, or lust, and I don't know why, except that I am going through a stage in my life when I'm not having any! Actually several people were outraged by that last story, by the fact that a 50-year-old woman and an 18-year-old boy could be attracted to each other, even though nothing comes of it.

I had known about paleontology already, but I do quite a lot of research for my writing, which I enjoy. But I think the thing I enjoy the most, not just in writing, but in the *world*, is the day when you do the first draft of a short story: when you have done the research, and you know you are going to do it, and I nearly always do the first draft in one go – which takes about six or seven hours, and is just *yes*! If you write like that, you have to do a lot of reworking. In a way, I prefer writing short stories to novels, because you cannot do that with a novel: it would take you 13 years! So novels are never quite as well muscled-out or well-worked as a short story. Apart from anything else, with a short story, you can remember everything you have got in it. With a novel you have ghastly things you can't remember, like which town you had this person at university in, and you have to go back and look it up.

I don't plot my novels, although I am quite proud of the structure of *Three Times Table*. The three lives parallel each other so tightly and yet are so different. But compared to the short stories, the novels are fairly ideological, about fairly abstract things. For instance, *Three Times Table* is about the power of the imagination; *Home Truths*, the one where a woman loses her hand, is about how feminists work and a kind of anti-psychotherapy book. In my books the themes are the most important thing, and the characters are made to fit the themes. When I teach creative writing, I often say that if a novel is well written, you shouldn't really know where the writer started and if it is a plot- or character- or idea-driven novel, or one of the few language-driven novels. I definitely start with an idea and construct both the story and the characters to illustrate that idea, whereas I know a lot of people start very strongly with the characters and the style grows out of that.

I keep a lot of notebooks, and I find the actual minute of starting, the writing of the first sentence, *unbelievably* difficult. I think it is because the story is perfect in your head and the minute you write the first line, it is never going to be perfect again. In order to crack that hurdle, I very often write the first three or four sentences somewhere not at my desk, and on a very scruffy bit of paper. After that I write straight onto a word-processor. I don't have a laptop, so the computer is always in the same place, and I feel the physical circumstances have to have a kind of magic about them.

If I am writing the first draft of anything, I increase the heat in the room. I turn up the radiator a couple of hours before I am going to do it – and I don't know why that is except that it is always warm. I have also discovered that there is a very precise degree of physical exercise that it works best if I take before I start: so I am not tired, but not restless. For me, that is usually walking now – but swimming would do just as well. In that sense, I am quite ritualized about it, although I like to pretend I am not. Now that I live on my own, I do not have a set schedule of when I am going to write. One of the nice things now, is that if I want to write in the afternoon, no one is going to come and ask, 'What's for supper Mummy?'

I do an awful lot of the writing before I start physically writing. You always get little surprises in the actual writing, but in terms of the plot, it is worked out in my head before. So it makes it quite difficult to say when I am working and when I am not. I might not have written for a whole week, but I would know that I had been working. My husband used to say that if I ever decided the house needed cleaning, it was when I ought to have been writing. I walk a lot now: and in a way, I see that as work. When I am really writing on the page, I tend to do it for seven or eight hours, but I don't keep that up for very long.

I have chosen to live on my own now, partly because it just happened, and partly because of religion: it is about praying. Now I have less inclination to write – which is a bit worrying, since God knows how I am going to keep myself in reclusivity. But what I really want to do is pray most of the time. I am working at the moment on a cultural history of silence, so some of it is very extensive research. I am absolutely fascinated by what happens when I am silent, even though, as you may have noticed, silence doesn't come very naturally to me!

The longest time I have achieved it was for six weeks. I managed by renting a house on Skye and taking all my food and a bread-making machine with me. My landlady delivered milk. I didn't speak or listen to any TV, or radio, or people. I found my other senses became more aware: like the taste and texture and smell of porridge was astounding. I am also a voice-hearer and I feel I was more receptive to that. Now I make my students sit in silence for two hours! It is a new hobby. But I am also interested in how it affects the imagination.

In the millennium year I was 50 and my youngest child left home. So three big events happened at once and I think I just wanted something new to do. I *loved* having children in the house; I liked them even more when they were adolescents. We had a very open-house policy. I was married for many years to a vicar, and good vicars, which he was, have very unboundaried lives, not private lives, and I really enjoyed it. But it had run out, and I wasn't interested in it any more. I was living in Northampton then, and my son was off to university, and I realized I didn't need such a big house and could live anywhere.

I am also not very good at pursuing a sensible career, so I never have very much money, and you can live very comfortably in a small house on top of a hill on the money I make. Essentially I am a lazy person, and on your own you don't have to cook for anybody, or clean the house, unless you want to. But the serious side of it is that I think prayer is the most interesting thing. Sometimes I feel that writing is just a way of developing that side of my imagination that enables that to happen.

I am not really ambitious any more, for rather a sad reason. I think success and merit in writing have now got so separated by what I think is a crap publishing culture. I cannot see that if I wrote as well as I can write, it would make me successful. I will sound like an elitist snob now, but for instance, the Booker short-list this year is *so* middlebrow. There is no chance for people not already established. I don't believe that Salman Rushdie's great books would be on a list now. I find it discouraging to think the best writers are not the ones to get their books published. The people whose work is taken up by agents are not, on the whole, the ones I feel are the best.

Nevertheless I am really enjoying teaching creative writing, and particularly, doing it online. I teach a distance-learning MA. I really enjoy my students, and that is very new. The whole pedagogy of creative writing surprisingly intrigues me, although I thought it wouldn't. I am just finishing a book about creative writing and I was surprised that I enjoyed writing that, too. I have become much more thoughtful about my own process. I don't think I would have done this interview with you a few years ago – I would have just written back saying really that is not my thing: it is all magic, which I don't want to talk about.

I am now just beginning to be fascinated by talking about what happens. I am very interested in the link between imagination and form – why some people are painters and others writers, and yet most people know from quite young which they want to do. Visual artists also know they want to be a sculptor rather than a painter. Where is the line between being a poet and a short-story writer; being a short-story writer and a novelist; being a novelist and a biographer? You choose instinctively. I think it has become clearer to me, because of how long I keep the whole thing in my head. What would happen if I worked the whole thing out and didn't write it, and what is actually going on? What changes the fundamental creativity that everybody has into an art form, really engages me.

There is some kind of natural talent. Some of my students, I know after the second assignment, are not going to hack it. Writing can get more competent, but may never catch fire. It is not a failure of their imagination: their ideas are just as good, and it is not a failure of craft, it is something else, even though that is unfashionable to think. The thing I am proud of in my own writing is the ability not to repeat myself. I know I, like everyone, have themes, and I am also guilty of self-satire, but I have done a very wide range of things, and hope to go on doing so. I never want anyone to say, 'The new Sara Maitland' as opposed to 'Sara Maitland has written another book'.

I have made a career on my own terms and don't feel compromised. I have been extremely lucky. The 70s were a very exciting time because of feminism, and I had my first child rather young, so I never had to go and get a proper job. I have always managed to live off writing-related work. Winning the Somerset Maugham award early on made my life possible. I got support, and the next three novels were commissioned before they were written, which gives you an amazing freedom. I began a writing career with an absolute confidence that I could do it, and it gave me contacts and connections, for instance at the BBC, which have meant I could always just manage to pay the mortgage.

I am no longer greedy about getting things published. I am writing a lot, but it is very experimental. For instance, in my latest collection of short stories, the one called 'Sybil' is much more language-based. I have also just written a story for a collection to be published in the north east, by north-eastern writers, called *Bound*. And again, this story is much less narrative: almost a meditation. St Cuthbert, who is the great saint of the north east, had an incorruptible body, and the story is a meditation about someone who is dead but whose body is still there, and how much he hates it. I wouldn't have any idea what to do with a story like that in any mainstream publishing, but that has stopped bothering me. I am writing things I wouldn't have written before, which is really exciting. 'My joyful curiosity still outweighs my fear.'

# Harry Mathews

*Harry Mathews is the only American member of the Oulipo, the Workshop for Potential Literature, France's longest-running and most active literary movement. It is a workshop that applies mathematical formulae, particularly algebraic methods of permutation and combination, to literature. It explores constrictive forms of writing, most famously as exemplified by Georges Perec's lipogrammatic novel,* La Disparition, *which never uses the letter 'e'. But Mathews believes that a consciousness of form is paradoxically liberating – freeing the unconscious, and forcing you to write in a way that you wouldn't do otherwise.*

*Certainly he has won many admirers. At a recent packed reading in London there was standing-room only remaining for his audience (which was not the usual middle-aged contingent, but included tattooed women and a man with bright blue hair). Esteem for his novel* Cigarettes *includes this from the* San Francisco Chronicle: 'Cigarettes *is Harry Mathews at his most brilliant and passionate, a tour de force by one of the most remarkable prose stylists presently writing in English.' Mathews writes with grace, humour, ingenuity, and an intriguing mix of artifice and reality. Among his awards is the Ordre des Arts et des Lettres, given by the French Government to honour his distinguished literary career and his services to French culture.*

*Born and raised on New York's Upper East Side, Mathews left America in 1952, shortly after graduating from Harvard, and has spent much of his adult life in France. He has co-edited the* Oulipo Compendium, *translated many works, written essays on literature and art, several volumes of poetry, and six novels. I talked to Mathews (who was both fascinating and charming) over the phone, from his house in Lans-en-Vercors, a village near Grenoble, which interestingly is the setting for the ending of his 'autobiographical' novel* My Life in CIA.

**Selected Bibliography**

Novels
*Tlooth* (1966), *Cigarettes* (1987), *The Journalist* (1994), *My Life in CIA* (2005)

Poetry
*The Ring* (1960), *Trial Impressions* (1977), *Out of Bounds* (1989)

Short Stories
*The Human Country* (2002)

Non-fiction
*20 Lines a Day* (1988, journal), *Oulipo Compendium* (1998, co-editor), *The Case of the Persevering Maltese* (2003 essays)

From the opening of *Cigarettes*:

'What's he mean, "I suppose you want an explanation"? He doesn't explain anything.'

The gabled house loomed over us like a buzzard stuffed in mid flight. People were still arriving. Through the lilac hedge came the rustle of gravel smoothly compressed, and swinging streaks of light that flashed beyond us along a pale bank of Japanese dogwood, where a man in a white dinner jacket stood inspecting Allan's letter with a penlight.

He passed the letter around. When it was my turn I read, in another revolution of headlights, '. . . the state I was in – barely seeing you when they were taking me away . . . Darkness, blinding light . . . I couldn't manage a squeak.' I too was confused. Even dazzled by Elizabeth, could this be Allan?

I wanted to understand. I planned someday to write a book about these people. I wanted the whole story.

\*       \*       \*

I chose this passage because it contains in it so much of what is going to happen later in the book, even though that might not be immediately obvious. For instance, there is an 'I' speaking there, who doesn't return until the last chapter of the book, and that retroactively changes the way the book has been read. He is a character who is curious about what the appearance of this letter signifies, and who wants to write about these people.

The majority of the novel is told in the third person, to induce the reader into the normal, complacent assumption that what he, or she, is reading is in fact what is happening. With the reappearance of the individual, who turns out to be a rather disreputable masochist homosexual, everything that one has read before is undermined, or at least has to be thought about again. This is something that happens in one way or another in every book I've written. There is a kind of sabotaging of the book that takes place, so that what one assumes has been happening is cast into question. The point of this is so that the reader realizes that the experience he or she has been having is one of reading a novel, and not reading about, or experiencing some reality that exists outside the book.

At the beginning you don't know what is going to happen or what this means, so it opens a lot of room for possibility. It is a way of starting a novel: to make the scene both vivid and confusing at the same time. It is also quite *film noir* in atmosphere, a medium which I admire enormously. I envy the fact that a movie can do in five seconds what it sometimes takes a lot of words to establish, and I think I was trying to get that done as quickly and efficiently as possible.

*Cigarettes* is my only fully Oulipian novel. Very often people will address me as an Oulipian writer, and I am not: I am an Oulipian and I am a writer – as are most of the members, with the possible exception of Georges Perec, who was Oulipian through and through in everything he did. The Oulipo is not really a literary movement, in that we don't think that following fairly strict forms is a better way to write than any other. All ways of writing are fine if they produce convincing results. Every Oulipian who is a member of the group engages in an exploration of possibilities confined to this rather specialized area of using very demanding or compelling ways to write, but that doesn't mean that we are going to do that. Most of the time, most of us don't write in an Oulipian manner, and that, to me, is very important.

Nevertheless, it is an extraordinary group. For one thing, it has been in existence for 45 years, which is something of a record for a group of this kind. We are not just writers, there are mathematicians and scholars amongst us, and most of the time, we all get along very well and have a very good time. We are really like a group of researchers who come together and compare notes on what we have been able to do. For me personally, Oulipian constraints are a way of liberating writing, but I am as reticent as I can get away with about exactly what methods I use.

There are really two points of view within the Oulipo: one is that adopted by Perec and Italo Calvino, for instance, which is to declare the procedures you use; the other approach, which I and Raymond Queneau adopted, believes that concealing the method used is more beneficial to a creative reading of the work than revealing what is there. I don't disagree with Calvino and Perec's point of view, but as Perec, alas, died so soon after publishing an explanation of the way he wrote *La Vie mode d'emploi* [(*Life: A User's Manual*)], people have written about that, rather than the book. [Generally acknowledged as a modern masterpiece. The lives of the inhabitants of 100 rooms are described in a Parisian apartment block in a sequence that follows the route a knight at chess would take to land on the 100 squares of a 10 x 10 chess board without landing on the same square twice. He also employed a mathematical formula called the 10 x 10 Greco-Latin bi-square to determine which theme would appear in each chapter.]

It is an extraordinary book, which I had to review when the English translation appeared, and I talked about the Oulipo, since Americans are largely unfamiliar with the group, but then I just talked about it as though it were the classical novel that it is. It is original, but does not need to be formally explained. If Georges were to have gone on living he would have told everyone to shut up when they kept going on about the formal procedures involved. I think all Oulipians feel that the procedures used to create the work become irrelevant once the print is on the page. People have asked me about the secret structure of my last book, *My Life in CIA*, and I say, 'First of all, if there is one, I am not going to tell you. Second, just read what is there, and see what happens when you read it.'

When there is an underlying hidden structure in a book, the reader, even if he has no idea what it is, soon becomes aware of it, and it gives an intensity to his reading that he wouldn't have otherwise. That it is the way I feel. As far as *Cigarettes* goes, no one is going to be able to figure out what the actual application of the procedure is. I have told people it is a permutation of situations, but they are so simple and so obvious that no one will be able to identify them. [On a simple level the novel is like a formal dance in which partners change from chapter to chapter.]

Its actual permutation was very challenging, and very hard to satisfy. I had plans laid out in front of me, which I stared at for a year, in between teaching and doing other things. Then gradually it filled itself up, as though I didn't have to do anything, but over a period of about eight years. It was very hard for me to write, but it was also extremely liberating in that it enabled me to write about the world I grew up in, which I had never been able to write about before, just as Perec's writing a book without using the letter 'e' brought him for the first time into touch with his own history of deprivation. [Jewish, Perec was orphaned at six: both parents killed in the war.]

I started writing because my parents, and my beloved maternal grandfather, all read to me when I was little: they read poetry, children's versions of *The Iliad* and *The Odyssey*, the Nordic Legends – quite exceptional stuff for a child of five or six. My mother was a passionate lover of Shakespeare, and of poetry. I remember one extraordinary moment when we were walking across 72$^{nd}$ street in Manhattan, and something I mentioned made her stop in her tracks and recite, 'O for a beaker full of the warm South, / Full of the true, the blushful Hippocrene, / With beaded bubbles winking at the brim, / And purple-stained mouth; / That I might drink, and leave the world unseen, / And with thee fade away into the forest dim' from the second stanza of Keats's 'Ode to a Nightingale'. And she quoted this with such passion – it was practically a sexual passion, and of course I was her beloved only child, and part of the flame caught me too.

I also had a wonderful teacher at school, an Englishman, Captain Fry, who was an enthusiast of Browning, of all people, as well as Wordsworth and Keats. So I had a lot of exposure to poetry, and that was what 'turned me on'. I think I wrote my first poem when I was 10 or 11, and gave it to Humphrey Fry, and I watched him as he read it, and when he put it down, he looked off into the distance, and to me, the look in his face was, 'My God, what have I done?' Because I was in a private school which was meant to prepare future professionals for their work, and I think he could tell from this poem that he might have got me started in a non-profitable direction.

Anyway, I began writing poetry then, and that was really all I wrote for many years. After the Romantics, my first inspirer, and the poet who introduced me to modernism, was T. S. Eliot. For a while, reading and writing poetry was the greatest passion of my life. Then I went to university, and after I had been there for a year and a half, it just stopped, and I felt it was just something that was nice while it lasted. Then I graduated, and a year later I began writing again, and I haven't stopped since then. At that time I was still in the kind of Eliot and Pound world, and it wasn't until I met John Ashbery, in 1956, that I realized I could do anything: I could indulge my wildest madnesses in writing, providing that it worked. All the poems that I have kept start from that time, when I was 26 years old, and I wish I had written more.

I still write poetry, but mainly because I love it so much, and I do it for fun, but I have never been serious about creating a public persona as a poet – not that I have created a public persona as anything, but I have neglected my poetry. I think poetry is the best possible training for a prose writer, because it rubs your nose into the actuality of language, but I wasn't able to write prose in any satisfying way until much later, and even then I struggled.

For instance, one of my aims in writing *Cigarettes* was to write a modernist novel, which on the surface would be as clear as Jane Austen, but really everything that happens in *Cigarettes* happens in the gaps between the chapters and even between paragraphs. I had to learn how to write what looked like a rather normal psychological novel, and it was the first time that I had gone into relationships: the hows and whys people react the way they do to one another. Before, I just let it happen, so it took me a long time to get it right, which I think I ultimately did. I had a very good reader, who was my first wife [Niki de Saint Phalle], who suffered the torments of the damned for having to tell me again and again, 'No this isn't any good.' She was a terrific reader, and I knew she was totally supportive of me, and I would get upset about her reactions, but then I would bless her for being honest with me. So she kept me on track until it worked out.

I do a lot of rewriting. I also have a detailed plan. In the case of *Cigarettes* I had an 80-page outline of the book. If you look at that book, it is impossible to imagine anything else, because just getting the dates right is a feat. It is like a detective story. *My Life in CIA* involved less formal working out, but I did a great deal of research on what was happening from day to day at that time [1973]. I mean, I couldn't remember when I saw a particular movie, whether it was 1973 or 1979, and so I went back and was able to put some of what I found into the general outline. I knew how the book would end, and I knew what the overall story would be, but I didn't work out the particular scenes, or anything like that, as I had in *Cigarettes*.

In *The Journalist*, my preceding book, I also left myself much more leeway. There was formal pattern, but the only Oulipian element was all the relationships, and the misunderstandings which arose between the various characters were worked out ahead of time. For any book I would do an outline first, but for me, what is interesting about fiction, or writing of any kind, is discovering what one doesn't know, or doesn't realize one knows. That is why it can properly be called creation. You are confronted with a hypothetical series of situations, and you don't know how to make them work.

What matters most to me is how the situations ultimately do work. All the other things, such as character, are just accessories to the crime! What matters to me is the reality of what happens on the page. This can take any form, like relationships between people, or an exciting event, all kinds of things, including (especially in my earlier books) word-play, which for me is never gratuitous: I always feel it has a very specific, and for me, potentially exciting effect as a presence.

As I said, at the end of each of my six novels, something happens which, in one way or another, throws everything that has happened into doubt. What I feel is my only moral obligation is to make every page real in whatever way is appropriate, and there is no way of predicting what that will be. It has to be real for the reader, and of course I am the reader, too: I just happen to be the first reader.

A writer doesn't communicate by getting his feelings down on paper. There is nothing wrong with that, but what good does that do if it is not going to be recognized and understood by the reader? So I feel that the way I communicate with the rest of the world is by joining the community of my own readers, and, of course, trying to give them enjoyment, however unpleasant the subject. I love reading Primo Levi! I am filled with a sense of life because of the way he uses his material in writing.

Writing is amazingly difficult, and while I am writing I am wondering whether there is going to be time for a drink! Although, actually, there are times when it comes easily. It took me a while to get there, but I do love writing. I really enjoy it, and that includes the knowledge that very likely what I have just written isn't going to survive my rereading of it. Ultimately it is a passion for a certain kind of truth, and it is not anything said in the words that I write. Words are out in the world of things, not inside us the way they feel, and so words can be said to be part of material reality.

But words can do certain things, and not other things. For instance they can very, very rarely solve practical problems of the world. There is probably a solution to every political problem in the globe that has already been written down, and is gathering dust in the Foreign Office, or some other similar place. Figuring out the answers doesn't do much good. What one can do in writing is make people aware of what the reality of words is, and what it isn't. Writing can be a fantastic reality and a very moving and exciting one, but it is also a very limited one, and that is one of the reasons I sabotage my own books. No matter what people's feelings were whilst reading the books, and their feelings probably included, 'When can I stop and have a drink?', it is a linguistic experience and not anything else.

Writing is not representational; it is not just a reflection of the world outside. Robert Louis Stevenson said this much better than me. I think I can find what he actually said very quickly. He wrote, 'The novel, which is a work of art, exists not by its resemblances to life, which are forced and material, as a shoe must still consist of leather, but by its immeasurable difference from life, which is designed and significant, and is both the method and meaning of the work.' So the shoe is made of leather and writing will talk about experiences or things that exist outside language, but it is very secondary.

I am interested in many forms of writing, for instance things like chronograms, which I wrote as prose. They were very, very hard and lots of fun to do. The chronogram is a very ancient form, or method, usually in verse. In a chronogram every letter corresponding to a Roman numeral [c, d, i, l, m, v, x] is counted and they are all added up and produce a specific date. For instance there are some houses in Brussels with a Latin text (the language is irrelevant) and the sum of the letters corresponding to the Roman numbers add up to the date of the building of the house. In my case I did it for the year I was in, 1998, and then did one for each year.

I made it extra difficult. Each one of my chronograms is two chronograms: there is the title, which is very short, just a few words, which add up to let's say the year 2000. Then there are pages of text, which also add up to 2,000. The only way of doing that is to exclude all the letters corresponding to Roman numerals except for i for 1. So for the year 2000, you have to have 2,000 i and no c, d, l, m, v, or x. So it is actually what is called a lipogram in Oulipian terms [a certain number of letters obligatorily left out]. It was very demanding and very engaging in both senses of the word.

As for poetry: the way I approached it did change after I became a member of the Oulipo, because I found all sorts of things that I could do that I hadn't thought of doing before, and which I didn't even try and hide. The procedures are there, out in the open. But from the beginning of time, the formal aspect of poetry has always been part of its meaning. Actually I wrote a series of very practical poems called 'Butter and Eggs' [almost like recipes] which I thought were absolutely not Oulipian. Then I realized, in a way, they were the most Oulipian thing one could do, which is to exclude all devices. So, in a sense, I invented what could be described as the ultimate Oulipian form in poetry, which was to have no formal requirements at all: no metre, rhyme, metaphor, imagery, or other method or device. And they were very well-received.

I write with a pen usually, a pencil sometimes. I transfer it to a computer later, and correct as I transfer, and then print it out, and do more corrections with a pen, or pencil. Then that is what is lovely about a computer: you can put your corrections in so easily. I usually write at my desk. I never thought of that before – Perec could write any place. I always dreamed of sitting in a Paris café and writing, but I don't do that. In my youth (the old man said) I would sit at my desk at 9 o'clock and work all morning, and part of the afternoon, but I am afraid I don't manage that any more.

I did have a period of horrendous procrastination that I would go through every day, so as to avoid rewriting *Cigarettes* for the third time. I was very reluctant to get to work, because I was having such a hard time, and was afraid of not being able to find the necessary improvement. So I would manage to dawdle, and shine my shoes, or do some weeding, or anything, and wouldn't get to work till five in the afternoon, which is a rather wasteful way to spend the day. Then I found this way of getting into the writing, which ended up as a book, although I had no idea it would become *20 Lines a Day*.

In fact I might go back to doing that exercise of writing something daily, because I have had a miserable time physically in the last few years with a herniated disc in my back. Now, I am much better, but I am a little bit in limbo at the moment. But I am translating my wife's [novelist, Marie Chaix] last book, which is the best of all writing exercises, I feel. When you start translating, even a relatively simple text, you think you know nothing about writing, but you realize you know less than nothing. It makes you really start thinking about basics.

I also want to get back to writing some more poems, and I have a couple of other assigned tasks that will get me going. And I do have a project for another novel, although it is still very nebulous. One of my plans right now is to learn about poetry all over again. I created my own personal anthology of English and American and a little bit of French poetry: quite small, starting with Skelton, and ending with poets who are younger than I am. I just want to see what has been going on through the centuries that I may not have been aware of: it is an exciting prospect. Please call me up and remind me to get started!

What I want to do in my novel writing is to give every sentence the density of poetry. It is not that the prose sentences should be poetic in any way, but that I should never be self-indulgent in writing any sentence of fiction. For instance, *My Life in CIA* is a book that seems to be very easy reading for most people, which is fine. But if you look at most of the sentences, they are as plain as plain could be, they are economical, they move things along and they are not gratuitous. It is a way of creating thought in writing. I tried, especially in that book, not to make anybody aware of what might be called style; I just wanted them to read. What matters is this recreation of thought, which is what keeps on going rapidly through the book.

I write with a *huge* amount of passion, and that's not meant to show. But to get those sentences right, one really has to care passionately about what one is doing, and I do. I am a devotee of classicism: whether it is Greek poetry, or certain modernist writers of the eighteenth century. That is to say, for me, expressionism doesn't work, and the direct expression of feelings is not the way to recreate them. Classicism works by putting a linguistic object in front of you, to which you react. That is not necessarily expressing an experience, but creating the possibility for the reader to recreate it. The basis of twentieth-century modernism was this realization that language had a life of its own, and it was through that life that you could engender realities other than information. I feel very passionately about life, and a little less passionately about my writing, and the way that they are connected is by working on the objective efficiency of the texts I write.

# Michael Morpurgo

*Born in St Albans during the Second World War, Michael Morpurgo is currently one of the best-known writers for children. He has written over 100 books, many of which have been winners of prizes worldwide. His children's stories vary from the historic* Joan of Arc *to the picturebook (filled with rhythm and alliteration)* Little Albatross – *both tackling social issues. He also writes his own libretti and screenplays and has edited anthologies. Michael Morpurgo was Children's Laureate (2003–5), attending readings, conferences and festivals. In addition, over 25 years ago, he and his wife founded the charity Farms for City Children: they now have three farms where children from towns come to experience life on a farm.*

*From all that I had read about Michael Morpurgo, I feared he might be 'too good to be true'. However I need not have worried. In conversation he was extremely interesting and was both considerate and sincere. He is brave to imbue his children's books with adult themes, and he has a genuine love of children and of storytelling. When I phoned to arrange the interview his wife answered and told me he was working. I offered to ring off, but she sought him out and he came to the phone to ask if I would mind phoning back at 6 pm when his writing day would be over.*

## Selected Bibliography

Children's Books

*Thatcher Jones* (1975), *War Horse* (1982), *Why the Whales Came* (1985, made into a film starring Helen Mirren), *King of the Cloud Forest* (1987), *The Dancing Bear* (1994), *Wreck of the Zanzibar* (1995), *The Butterfly Lion* (1996), *Camelot: The Last Days* (1998), *Wombat Goes Walkabout* (1999), *Out of the Ashes* (2001), *Private Peaceful* (2003), *Adolphus Tips* (2005)

From the opening of *Private Peaceful*:

### Five Past Ten

They've gone now, and I'm alone at last. I have the whole night ahead of me, and I won't waste a single moment of it. I shan't sleep it away. I won't dream it away either. I mustn't, because every moment of it will be far too precious.

I want to try to remember everything, just as it was, just as it happened. I've had nearly eighteen years of yesterdays and tomorrows, and tonight I must remember as many of them as I can. I want tonight to be long, as long as my life, not filled with fleeting dreams that rush me on towards dawn.

Tonight, more than any other night of my life, I want to feel alive.

*       *       *

The way in which I begin a book is very important because it sets up the *voice* that you choose. I tend to often write in the first person – about two-thirds of my books are written in the first person. I tend to *become* the person who is telling the story, the central character is me, so in a way, I have to climb into this character before I ever set pen to paper. Those lines from *Private Peaceful* flowed remarkably easily. I knew that there were going to be two tones: the immediate tone of the soldier, me, sitting in a barn waiting for his brother to be shot at dawn; and this reflection which forms the majority of the book, of him thinking back, retelling his life to himself in order to postpone dawn. So the whole way in which the book is designed is in those first few paragraphs.

I think of the voice first, and from that, the structure. In this particular case, I knew that it was going to be told in the first person, as because of the subject, it seemed very important to me that you were as close to the heart of this matter as possible. Then I was looking at my watch one morning, and thought, 'This surely is the way to do it. A man waiting for his brother to die would look at his watch frequently, and that might be my chapters, and that would be a way of bringing the reader, and indeed me, back to another time.' I am a very lucky writer. I tend to wait until the good idea happens, and when it does, the voice comes with it or just before it. All this is quite difficult to explain, because I am a very unsystematic writer. I don't plot, or plan: I tend to dream things out and trust to my instinct when I sit down. What I try to do when I write a story is not to write it at all, but to tell it.

I think a confusion comes when people think that writing for children is different from writing for anyone else. For *me* it is absolutely not. I tend to write stories about what it is that perplexes me – what I am still curious, worried, angry, fascinated about. I am not trying to teach children through my books, but am concerned with teasing out an issue or a problem, and examining it in terms of story to see where it takes me. That is how I deal with things – with old age, for instance, now. A lot of my books are about relationships between younger people and older people: I have got six grandchildren.

I write what I care to write about, and having been a teacher is only relevant in that I learnt then that you never talk *down* to children. Children can take any subject you wish to throw at them without any problem at all. They don't lack intelligence or perception: they lack experience. That is it. So that way in which I talked to children is still there in my writing, but I don't want to ram messages home. I hope there are messages, but they may be different from the message that the book has for *me*. I just write and I hope that my books affect adults as well as children.

I have lived and worked all my life with children. I *know* children really well: they are my planet. I was a father at the age of

19 and now I am a grandfather. I was a teacher for ten years and I have been running this project at the farm, where 1,000 children come here every year. My world is peopled with children. They interest and fascinate and irritate me. And a writer writes, generally speaking, about the landscape which he knows. And in the doing of that, I people my stories with characters who interest me, which seem to be children and old people.

I have lived a kind of double life: a very physical life out on the farm for the last 25 or 30 years, with the children. I am not strictly there working as a farmer; I am working with *them*. And all the time I am *gathering* impressions of children – what they are saying to one another, how they respond to the animals, to the work, to the weather, to the teacher. So I am in a very privileged position where I can observe them at close quarters, and indeed, relate to them. I think that is probably at the heart of it. If you were to say to me, 'Would you like to go out farming on your own, and work the land and work the beasts?' the answer would probably be, 'No'. Particularly now; I am too tired.

But at the time I was doing it, it was very invigorating because for *me*, each day on the farm was like a great book for the children. At the beginning of the day you were opening a book and the story of that day for me and for the children was something that we both don't forget, because remarkable things happen. If I had to choose between writing, or farming with the children, the one is *real*, and so it would probably be the farming. I think writers can get very involved with their own self-importance. We are basically, including Shakespeare, storytellers. We tell tales and hope that they resonate with people, deeply. They are important, but life is important too, and living and relationships – the real thing and not simply recording or interpreting it. I believe very strongly that you cannot write as a young person, or indeed as an older person, unless you have a richness of experience to draw from. So the living comes before the writing as far as I am concerned.

I started writing when I was about 26, whilst I was still teaching. First I was encouraging the children I was teaching to write, and I read a wonderful book called *Poetry in the Making*, by Ted Hughes, which is really an invitation to everyone, saying, 'You can all do this. You have but to open your eyes, and feel and touch and be aware', and that has been my credo ever since. So I never made children write dry. We always went out and were stimulated and then we would come back and read poetry, or listen to music, or whatever, and then get into writing. I got into it because I was getting them to write and I thought, 'I can't sit here like a "dumbo", watching them'. So when we read out our poems or stories, I would read out mine. Also, at the end of each day, instead of reading them a story, I would *tell* them a story. And if I could – I didn't always succeed – I would try to make it so exciting that when the bell rang, they wanted more the next day. So I would go on, and tell a sort of 'soap'. So in a way I trained myself as a storyteller in order to fascinate children about stories.

I didn't plan these stories in advance, although I had ideas and notions that I would lie in bed and think about. I am a bit of an insomniac, which helps. So the night before, I would try and weave one or two things together. But rather like my books now, I would come to the blank page, or to the classroom, rather unprepared, and not knowing how it would finish. Almost every book I have written, I don't know the ending when I start. The ending is told to me by the characters and evolves and develops, and when I am writing at my best, that is what happens. When I was younger, I thought I had to impose myself upon stories; I had to make everything happen. But what happens then is that it becomes predictable. So as the confidence grows, you allow the story and the people in it to take control. I don't pull the strings. I watch it all happen and record it.

I write for many reasons, some of them quite boring and silly – very often because someone asks me to write something.

They might say, 'I want a short story of yours for a book, or some poems, or would you do a retelling of . . . ?' And very often I am very sparked by the *flattery* of someone asking me to do something, which sounds rather silly, but the notion that people *think* I can retell *Sir Gawain and the Green Knight* is wonderful, and enables me to think that I *can* do it. But over and beyond that, I have become almost an obsessive storyteller. So when I have finished telling a story, there seems to be one waiting to be told. For the last 20 years, that has always been the case. I have never been without a story in my head to dream about.

I have never had writer's block. I am very disorganized, and not particularly hard working, so if anyone were to get writer's block, it should be me. But the reason I don't, I think, is because I live this very full and interesting life where I meet lots of people and go to lots of places and do lots of things. I also draw on my memory enormously, on things that happened to me when I was young. The funny thing is that the more that I draw on it, the more there seems to be there – things you think you have forgotten. Somehow by drawing water up, more water seems to come.

I tend to write on my bed – always somewhere where I'm comfortable. I used to write sitting at any desk, it didn't matter where it was. But because I get excited when I am writing, if it is going well – I want to almost get ahead of the story – my writing gets smaller and smaller and smaller. I write by hand on little notebooks, exercise books actually, which they give me in primary schools when I visit. My wife then transfers everything to a computer, bless her, she is doing that now as we are talking. I tried. I lost five chapters of a story about six years ago, and have never trusted computers ever since, and I have gone back to writing by hand.

What it does is give me terribly bad pain in my neck and my shoulder. Two wonderful writers, my two mentors, solved my problem. The first person was Ted Hughes, who I got to know very well, and who helped to set up Farms for City Children. He said he had had the same problem, and that he stood at an easel to write. Well, I tried that, but my feet ached, so that wasn't any good. Then I looked at a photograph in a biography of Robert Louis Stephenson, who is the person I most want to be, and it was of him in Samoa, sitting on a bed, with his knees drawn up in front of him, and a great bank of pillows behind him, and he looked completely relaxed. So I thought, 'I'll try that' and it works. I have been writing like that now, sitting on a bed, for about ten years.

I can write in a train or aeroplane, I am not that bothered. What I do need is the *time* to dream it up beforehand. That is really important, and then I walk the lanes a lot around here. I dream about it in my bath, driving, it doesn't really matter, but the dream time – which is what I call it – takes certainly 75 per cent of my 'writing' time. It is not writing at all: it is trying to weave it together in my head so that it comes to some kind of rather amorphous mass from which I will draw my story when I sit down and write it. And as I said, the voice seems to emerge, and the voice gives shape to the mass. That's how it seems to happen.

The time the whole process takes doesn't seem to change much if the story I am writing is long or not. My short stories tend to be rather like poems and take just as long as a short novel. My novels generally take about six months of dreaming and six months of writing. I do five or six drafts and am very open and susceptible to editorial comment. My wife is my first editor. She tells me whether I am onto a loser, in which case, I go on to something else – but she has never said that. What she tends to do is to give little nudges saying, 'Maybe try this, or try that.' I do rely on editors quite a lot. I write fast, so I make mistakes. I do a lot of research. It is very important to get the research *right*, and that is all part of the dream time really.

Being the Children's Laureate has tended to stop me writing, which is fine, because I knew it would. It is two years of talking about books and writing about them and trying to inspire people to do their own writing and also to become interested in reading. I travel massively, reading stories to people, and trying to bring the story back into literacy. My main concern and worry at the moment is that we have a situation where books are simply used in the classroom to score points off, to answer questions from. But they were never written for that, and I think the love of books, and the listening to stories, and the music in your head when you hear a wonderful poem, should come first, before any study.

So I am trying to persuade people that the reason so many children are hacked off with reading, and don't want to do it, is very often because they see it as something you do at school and which is expected of you. Each Children's Laureate has taken their own particular platform, and that has been mine. Quentin Blake did a wonderful thing about illustration, and Anne Fine did a lot about book owning and libraries, and mine is about the sheer enjoyment of stories and storytelling.

When I write stories I don't have anyone in particular in mind. I am writing for *me*. The most important person to keep amused is me. If I can't entertain me, and keep me focused, then it isn't any good. I must be fascinated and completely wound up in it. I must cry, or howl with laughter, and live through whatever the characters are going through. What I can't do is write a book like *Private Peaceful* and then write another one. I can't be a Pat Barker [who wrote a trilogy of novels about the First World War], in other words. I cannot go on with themes that I have suffered through. I need to escape from them and go to something completely different.

That is why I write picturebooks and retellings and all the rest of it. I think I am pretty much a compulsive writer now, but what I do like is being *fresh* for every book, and each book is a completely new challenge: a different time in history, a different kind of story – magical or with a strong social background. Publishers try to encourage you to do the same sort of thing again with a bit of a difference, but that doesn't interest me at all. That is why I am difficult to sell. If you write like Agatha Christie, you can sell one book after another, and the same thing with Jacqueline Wilson. I am not saying all the books are the same. But they have a way of being, and cover a sort of ground, which everyone understands, and you can build up a sort of library that way. I really admire people who can sustain that, just as I admire people who write a trilogy, but I absolutely couldn't. When I have done a novel I want to leave that world and go somewhere else.

I am not proud of anything in my own writing, but I do love the feeling that a story works. There is a wonderful moment when you are reading a story to an audience, whether it is 5, or 500, when there is an extraordinary intensity of silence which happens. For me, that is in a way the greatest joy. You know that everyone in that room is living, now, within your story, each in their own way, each having their own vision of whatever it is you have invented. I love that. I love the feeling of leaving an audience gasping at the end. That is really what I am trying to achieve.

If there is pride in it, it is that, not seeing my name on the outside of a book. There has just been a wonderful play of *Private Peaceful* and there is a brilliant intensity of the actor in this particular performance, and people are just stunned by it and he, too, must get this wonderful feeling. It is power to a degree. You feel you have had these people in the palm of your hand. If as a storyteller, without great acting ability, I can do that, then it makes me feel that it is worthwhile and worth writing the next one.

It is flattering if someone wants to do a play or film from one of my books, but the caveat, and I have learnt this to my own cost, is that you must find people who are in sympathy with the spirit of it. With one or two of the films that have been made of my books that has not been the case. With drama, however, I have been very lucky. In each case I have come across wonderful adaptors and directors who have caught the spirit of it and really made it sing in their particular medium. And I love seeing something have another, altogether different life; that gives me a lot of joy.

Similarly, it is hugely important to get the right illustrator for a picturebook. In exactly the same way, if you get the wrong illustrator, the whole tone of the book is changed, whereas if you get the right one, the whole thing is not only enhanced, but it becomes again a different thing: a book of illustrations and story, not simply an illustrated story. I think the problem is that so many illustrations tend to simply echo something in the book rather than adding something. Michael Foreman, whom I work with most, has an instinct for getting under the skin of a story and knowing its colour and the feeling of pace and excitement. You don't have to tell him anything, which is wonderful. I have also just done a collection of Aesop's Fables illustrated by Emma Chichester-Clark, and again you can see the exquisite joy she had in doing it, and it lifts the stories from being, in fact slightly repetitive, to each one being very special and jewel-like.

I don't actually decide on the age group of the readers of the story, or whether it will be illustrated, in advance. I think that is one of the reasons editors have problems with me. They constantly say, 'Children that young don't like that sort of thing.' I wrote a book called *The Silver Swan*, which was about a swan who is killed by a fox, and indeed in *Little Albatross*, there is a picture of a killer-bird coming down – and a child looking at that in bed at night is going to be startled by it, which is fine, and what I want. I would rather just write the story and hope that it works. Sometimes they don't, and they sit in my little cupboard.

Last Christmas I wrote a short story for *The Big Issue*, and I thought, 'Well, it will have a terrible illustration with it.' But then it was put in the *Guardian* or the *Sunday Times* – I can't remember – with an equally bad illustration, and suddenly a publisher said, 'We want to make a picturebook out of this.' And they made a picturebook out of it, with Michael Foreman doing the drawings, and I think it is the kind of picturebook which both adults and children will read. It is a story about the Christmas trees in the First World War. It is coming out this Christmas, and I know from people's reactions already that it will be a marvellous little illustrated book, but it wasn't designed in the first place to be such a thing: it was just designed as a short story. Some other writers, like Paul Gallico, for instance, wrote short stories which appeared in places like the *New Yorker*, and ended up as illustrated short stories, and even movies, which I am sure he didn't intend at first. I am a bit like that. I tend to simply write the story and hope.

I do recognize recurring themes in my writing, like animals and people's relationships with them, which comes from my observations of my own children and grandchildren and the children down on the farm. I see how one gives confidence to the other and trust. War is another thing which has been part of my life ever since I can remember, because I was born in 1943 and my first memories were of Blitzed London. The adults all talked about this thing that had happened, which of course I hadn't lived through, so I was rather fascinated by it.

There were photographs of my dead uncle on the mantelpiece. He was shot down in the RAF and I never knew him, but he was hailed as a hero by my family, so I always had terrific respect, and love indeed, for this Uncle Peter of mine. I had never met the man but I adored him. There he was, just a black and white photograph – he stayed the same all his life. So I could see in the adults around me, this whole business of what the war did to people like my mother and stepfather. In fact my mother and father were split up by the war, so the damage to buildings and the damage to people has been part of who I am. And war, and damage of all sorts, have been themes in my writing.

The process of writing for everyone is different, that is what is lovely about it. I don't really understand it, or ever claim that I do, but I am fascinated by the whole way it happens. One day I look at an empty piece of paper, and a week later I have written a short story, or a play, or whatever. I constantly marvel how the thing happens. What I do know, very surely, is that for me, it is almost like an instinct. I think I am looking for stories all the time, without even knowing that I am looking for them. Because of that, I think, interesting things seem to happen out of the blue.

For example, I was writing a story called *Billy the Kid*, and the reason I wrote it was because Michael Foreman said, 'Would you write a story about football?' I didn't want to write a story about football, but I thought about it, and I went to see a match at Chelsea with him, and began to be interested in this whole notion of why it is that people love this game so much, and why people were passionate about their team all their lives – which I had never been. So I was fascinated as a newcomer, and I invented this story about a footballer, a young man who loved Chelsea because his father did. His father was gassed in the First World War and the son ends up as being this wonderful young player. But his career is cut short by the Second World War and he has to go off to fight and everything goes wrong with his life.

I didn't know how to end this book. I knew he was going to go through this terrific trial and a slough of despond. His girlfriend is killed, and his family's house is bombed and he ended up being in the first ambulance that drove into Belsen and he gets wounded in the leg, and all these things, bit by bit, mean that he simply can't be the person that he was before the war. He is basically hugely damaged when the war ends, so he becomes a tramp. I had got this all sort of in my head, and he drank too much etc., but I had no idea at all where all this was going to go.

Then I went to Provence in France and I was sitting at a table having dinner with someone who ran the Aix-en-Provence Festival, at which I had been speaking, and she leant across the table at this wonderful inn, and said, 'I want to introduce you to my husband, but actually I live with two men.' So I said, 'What do you mean?' And she told me this story. She had been building her house, 30 years before, and they couldn't afford a builder, so she and her husband used to go at weekends and build it themselves on the hillside outside Aix en Provence. One day they arrived and they had just built the *cave* and they found this old bloke lying there surrounded by blankets and bottles.

They were nice young people so they didn't say, 'Push off' and the bloke said 'Hello' and offered them a drink, and they got to know one another and he said, 'I'll help you if you like. I'll sort some wood, and put some bricks on and make sure no one comes and damages the place . . .' Anyway, five years later the house was built, and by now he was living in the sitting-room. They didn't know what to do, because he was their great friend now, but one day they said, 'Henri, we need to move in. That is what we built the house for.' And Henri said, 'It is very simple. You build me a hut at the bottom of the garden and I'll move in there.' And that is what happened. He moved into the bottom of the garden and he was still drinking and they looked after him and he looked after them.

This whole story was told to me at the very moment I was looking for a resolution to this story of an old alcoholic tramp. It is that kind of serendipitous thing that I think is wonderful. But you don't find it unless you open yourself up to it. It is the business of being out there and keeping your heart open and your eyes open and, I think actually, it is keeping the child in you alive. It seems to me that is very important for any writer, it doesn't matter who you are writing for. So I've ended on a story. That's the way I like to do it.

# Joyce Carol Oates

*Joyce Carol Oates is one of the most respected and prolific authors in the United States, writing novels, plays, poems and criticism. She was born in 1938, and attended a rural one-room schoolhouse, before going to Syracuse University on scholarship. She then received her MA in English from the University of Wisconsin, where she met and married her husband. The couple settled in Detroit, and from 1968 to 1978 Oates taught in Canada, just across the Detroit River. Since then she and her husband have lived in Princeton, New Jersey.*

*Oates's novels, though greatly varied, are often characterized by her protagonist's struggles to define themselves against oppressive environments, sometimes involving extreme violence. Praise for her work includes these comments: 'Oates is a massive literary heavyweight', Guardian; 'Writing of unearthly brilliance', Sunday Telegraph; 'Not many authors – much less a female – could write about sex from the male point of view with as much relish and canniness', Philadelphia Inquirer; 'An inspired writer, and a formidable psychologist', Independent; 'Raw and rapid prose that is both disturbing and compelling', New Statesman; 'Joyce Carol Oates is a genius', Guardian.*

*A recipient of the National Book Award and the PEN/Malmud Award for Excellence in Short Fiction, member of the American Academy of Arts and Letters, Oates is the Roger S. Berlind Distinguished Professor of the Humanities at Princeton University. As well as teaching, she writes two or three books a year, and when I faxed questions for this interview, her answers arrived the next day. When I approached Joyce Carol Oates (by letter) she asked me (in an email) to fax her the questions, saying she would fax back the answers. She is the only writer in this book to whom I have not talked, but she gave her time generously. What follows is her written response. Very occasionally, to make the sense clear, I have added a few words of my questions at the start of paragraphs, and to make the interview flow I have altered the order.*

## Selected Bibliography

Novels
*With Shuddering Fall* (1964), *them* (1969), *Bellefleur* (1980), *Black Water* (1992), *What I Lived For* (1994), *Zombie* (1995), *We Were The Mulvaneys* (1996), *Blonde* (2000), *Rape: A Love Story* (2003), *The Falls* (2004), *The Stolen Heart* (2005)

Short Stories
*By the North Gate* (1963), *The Poisoned Kiss* (1975), *Heat and Other Stories* (1991), *The Collector of Hearts: New Tales of the Grotesque* (1998)

Poetry
*Anonymous Sins* (1969), *Tenderness* (1996)

Plays
*Miracle Play* (1974), *New Plays* (1998)

Non-fiction
*Edge of Impossibility: Tragic Forms in Literature* (1972), *On Boxing* (1987), *The Faith of a Writer: Life, Craft, Art* (2003)

From the opening of *Rape: A Love Story*:

> After she was gang-raped, kicked and beaten and left to die on the floor of the filthy boathouse at Rocky Point Park. After she was dragged into the boathouse by the five drunken guys – unless there were six, or seven – and her

twelve-year-old daughter with her screaming *Let us go! Don't hurt us! Please don't hurt us!* After she'd been chased by the guys like a pack of dogs jumping their prey, turning her ankle, losing both her high-heeled sandals on the path beside the lagoon. After she'd begged them to leave her daughter alone and they'd laughed at her. After she'd made the decision, Christ knows what she was thinking, to cross through Rocky Point Park instead of taking the longer way around, to home. To where she was living with her daughter in a rented row house on Ninth Street around the corner from her mother's brick house on Baltic Avenue. Ninth Street was lighted and populated even at this late hour. Rocky Point Park was mostly deserted at this late hour. Crossing the park along the lagoon, a scrubby overgrown path. Saving ten minutes, maybe. Thinking it would be nice to cross through the park, moonlight on the lagoon, no matter the lagoon is scummy and littered with beer cans, food wrappers, butts. Making that decision, a split second out of an entire life and the life is altered forever.

*       *       *

I asked to do this interview by fax, rather than over the phone, because obviously I am a writer, not a professional 'talker'. Language is my tool of choice, as, when I sit at the piano, as an enthralled amateur, the piano is my musical instrument of choice, exuding an air of mystery and beauty even when its keys are untouched.

My background is rural upstate New York, a girlhood spent on a small and not very prosperous farm. I think of myself as an 'American writer', tackling American topics, like most of my writer-friends who are Americans. But I began writing when I was a very young child and was enchanted by Lewis Carroll's wonderful Alice books.

I keep a journal, but very casually. I began in 1971 and have continued through the years, storing most of the material in archives of my work at Syracuse University. This is partly a writer's journal and partly a diary and frequently includes letters of mine.

I write my books initially in longhand, accumulate many pieces of paper, then convert the material into typed form via a typewriter with a word-processor and ten-page memory. It isn't a computer, yet it isn't an old-fashioned typewriter. It's a machine with which I feel comfortable. I can write at any time, preferably in the morning. Except when I'm travelling, I usually write in the same place, and I can work through much of the day with a good deal of interest and fascination.

Rewriting is my way of writing, a constant and usually quite engrossing process. If I could write 'perfectly' the first time, the way Mozart is said to have composed his music, I would feel letdown, disappointed. For, to me, rewriting/revising/reimagining is the very life's blood of the creative enterprise.

'Forbidden passions' are likely to be the fuel for writing. For most people these are the darker emotions: anger, hurt, envy, spite, rage, self-loathing, despair, lack of generosity, lack of a sense of community, indifference, deliberate stupidity. My characters range through all of these, and more.

Character, plot, language, image, all seem to arise at more or less the same time, as if materializing out of the void. For *The Falls* [a story of a family in crisis confronting their personal history against a background of scandal involving radioactive waste], the several characters, with whom I felt a strong emotional bond, are very much of 'The Falls' – that specific place, Niagara Falls, near where I grew up, and that time in our history – the notorious Love Canal environmental litigation case (1950s–1977 and beyond). For *Blonde*, the initial image was a photograph of the 17-year-old Norma Jean Baker taken some years before she was given the name 'Marilyn Monroe' – a very pretty, brunette-haired high school girl with little resemblance to the synthetic blonde actress she would be molded into within a few years. Without this initial image, glimpsed by chance, I would never have even considered writing *Blonde*.

For *Blonde* I saw each of Marilyn Monroe's films that are available through video rentals, in chronological order, which allowed me to observe the young actress maturing in her craft; I read several biographies, but chose to avoid the more controversial conspiracy-theory books that followed Monroe's death. In other words, I kept my research to a minimum, knowing that I would be imagining an interior life for my subject, which the 'exterior' life can only suggest. For the more recent *The Falls*, I supplemented my memory with research. Otherwise, my novels don't require formal research to any degree worth noting.

Most writers transform autobiographical material into fiction, often in elliptical and ingenious ways. We are all 'emotional' memoirists; otherwise, there would be little motivation for writing. But only in my novel *I'll Take You There* do I evoke the experiences and thinking of a protagonist similar to myself. Much of the novel is fiction, but a good deal – setting, atmosphere, specific scenes, the protagonist's predilection for philosophy while a student at Syracuse University in the 1960s – is directly based upon my own experience, and the narrative voice is identical with my own.

As a formalist, questions such as different structures and narrative voices are exciting and challenging to me. I love to vary points of view, ways of telling stories, the uses of language. Most of my writing is 'psychological realism' but I am drawn occasionally to other, more experimental modes. *Blonde* was my American 'tragic epic' and I doubt that I would undertake such a project again. *What I Lived For* was another 'tragic epic' with the model of James Joyce's *Ulysses* dimly in the background.

The general outline of a novel always exists for me, in the way of a road map, before I begin a novel. I usually have the very ending, the title, dominant images, crucial scenes. Of course, in the process of the writing, day by day and hour by hour, much is open to modification and improvisation. This is the excitement of any art! Everything I write is so many times rewritten, sometimes entirely reshaped, its final form is likely to differ considerably, in its nuances and details, from its initial form.

I write in several genres. The novel is the most challenging in terms of stamina; the novella, in terms of economy. Short stories are 'easier' for me psychologically since the genre is so open, fluid, experimental. But I love plays as well, the human voice in its myriad aspects. I love to read poetry but have virtually ceased writing it. And essays and reviews are enormously rewarding, a kind of relaxation after the rigors of writing in the mediated voice of fiction.

I have written a few novels using a pen name to assume anonymity, so precious to a writer. My new pseudonym, Lauren Kelly, writes more sparely than Joyce Carol Oates, in a genre that might be called 'psychological suspense'. It's interesting that you should suggest that some of my novels or novellas have a 'masculine' tone. I can't comment, really; I think of writing as gender neutral. I grew up surrounded by men, especially strong-willed men like Corky Corcoran [a wheeler-dealer womanizer in *What I Lived For*] who has learned to disguise his more sensitive self beneath a charismatic 'masculine' persona. I feel absolutely sympathetic with my male characters, even those whom others might dislike.

I also can't write unless I know the landscape/cityscape/atmosphere/often the history of the setting. My characters emerge out of their places, and represent them to a degree. I have a strong visual imagination, and often hope to convey, through language, not so much a 'cinematic' vision as one that is natural to an observing subject. It's as if, I would hope, the reader is physically/visually present in my fiction. But I've never thought of an audience for my writing per se. I'm usually quite absorbed in the way in which the integrity of the material is best displayed; what we mean by saying a story is 'fully realized' and not slighted or overblown. There is a certain hidden gravitas in any situation which requires rendering in the most skillful of ways, and it's this gravitas that fascinates me, not any particular audience for it. (In fact, there may be none!)

From my perspective, I have a prevailing sympathy for victims, often women and children, of violent acts perpetrated, often, by men; but I don't believe that I write anything like propaganda. I have an abiding interest, perhaps grounded in my background as a child surrounded by so many individuals who were not educated, were quite poor and politically disenfranchised, in bearing witness for those unable to tell their own stories. My young adult novels (*Big Mouth & Ugly Girl*, *Freaky Green Eyes*, *Sexy*, and the upcoming *After the Wreck I Picked Myself Up Spread My Wings and Flew Away*) deal precisely with moral/ethical subjects in ways that seem to me relevant to young people for whom idealism is instinctive.

In my most recently published novel, *Missing Mom*, retitled *Mother, Missing* in the UK, I examine close-up the effect of her mother's sudden death upon a woman of 31 who has imagined herself quite independent and in no way a typical 'daughter'. The predominant theme is perhaps the evolution of another, deeper self out of the seemingly settled, somewhat superficial self which many of us inhabit comfortably when our lives proceed without notable incidents or upsets.

I believe that serious art is transgressive: it provokes, it sometimes upsets, it causes us to think and not merely to acquiesce to pre-existing beliefs and platitudes. Serious art, too, isn't just about its content, but 'about' its formal principles as well: structure, tone, language, genre-types.

Whilst writing I go through a fairly full range of emotions, but especially frustration/doubt/irritation that the writing isn't going more smoothly. Running is my meditative time, without which I would feel very confined and lost. However, walking and bicycling and dancing can be equally wonderful. My 'feelings' are erratic and fluctuating but not very important, ultimately. Of course, I have difficult days, even quite discouraging days, but there is no question but that I will persevere, and finish any project I begin. The analogy might be with practising a musical instrument: even if you are naturally gifted as a musician, you must spend hours practising. There are no shortcuts. Since I began writing in the 1960s, my prose has become ever more complex and varied; my subjects often larger, 'metaphorical'. I am now assembling, by my editor Daniel Halpern's request, a massive book of stories – *High Lonesome: New and Selected Stories 1966–2006*. Beyond that, a novel titled *Black Girl, White Girl* set in 1972.

Pride isn't a value for me. I would be hard pressed to think of anything I am proud of except perhaps some of my former students who have gone on to publish acclaimed books, like the recent Princeton graduate Jonathon Safran Foer. I seem to be enormously ambitious in terms of individual projects, like the long, complex novels *Blonde, What I Lived For, Bellefleur*. I've never felt inordinately ambitious in terms of a career and have surprised associates by my lack of interest in 'promoting' myself, especially internationally. Though I'm often invited to attend literary conferences and festivals, and to visit foreign countries where my books are published, I virtually never accept.

I concur with Henry James. Writing is basically a mystery, as he put it, 'We work in the dark – what we can – we give what we have. Our doubt is our passion, and our passion is our task. The rest is the madness of art.'

I chose the opening lines from *Rape: A Love Story*, because they represent the generally spare, stripped-down narrative of the novella which presented itself to me as a problem in technique: how to condense a story to its primary features, using short chapters narrated in a 'poetic'-vernacular voice and limiting the novella to only a few characters and the plot to a strictly observed time-line. Everything in *Rape: A Love Story* follows from the initial sentence. The opening was imagined as a single paragraph, a torrent of long pent-up words uttered by the daughter of the rape victim, now a mature woman herself looking back upon this terrible interlude in their lives. In novels, certainly in my more customary novels, there is a semblance of 'life' in its multiplicity and complexity, its waywardness and dis-unity; but the novella is a form strict as a sonnet, challenging and gratifying to attempt.

Writing is a kind of conscious dreaming. As a formalist, as I said, I'm fascinated by the forms literature can take, the myriad ways in which a story can be told. Like dreaming, my writing is both enriching and a necessity; one is 'compelled' to dream, one has no choice. Something of the same is probably true for me though I have never attempted to go very long without writing.

# Don Paterson

*Don Paterson was born in Dundee in 1963. He left school at 16 to become a musician and still works as a jazz guitarist as well as writing poetry, editing and teaching. He started writing poems at 21, and then read obsessively, even including the entire dictionary (which I feel is sometimes evident in his work!). He won an Eric Gregory Award in 1990 and went on to win most of the major poetry prizes, including the T. S. Eliot and the Whitbread.*

*Paterson's poetry displays great formal dexterity with metre that is not rigid but is perceptible, and rhyme or more often half rhyme skilfully deployed. His poems are witty, at times cynical, lyric and challenging. He has been called 'the leading poet of his generation', while A. S. Byatt wrote: 'the life, energy, verbal precision and inventiveness of Don Paterson's* Landing Light *kept me awake at night. It changes my view of the whole landscape of British poetry for the better.' Paterson lives in Kirriemuir with his partner, three stepchildren and twin sons.*

*I met Don Paterson in 2002 when he was my tutor on an Arvon Foundation residential poetry course in a remote croft in Moniack Mhor. I gained from his erudition but found, as I suspect he did too, the intensity of the course rather a strain. Talking with him about his own work two years later he was still astonishingly articulate, but he seemed more relaxed and less formidable – in fact very modest.*

## Selected Bibliography

Poetry
*Nil Nil* (1993), *God's Gift to Women* (1997), *The Eyes* (1999), *Landing Light* (2003)

The final three stanzas from 'The Landing':

   and with as plain a stroke I knew
   I let each gutstring sound
   and listened to the notes I drew
   go echoing underground

   then somewhere in the afternoon
   the thrush's quick reply –
   and in that instant knew I'd found
   my perfect alibi

   No singer of the day or night
   is lucky as I am
   the dark my sounding-board, the light
   my auditorium

*    *    *

I chose these lines because, whether or not they are successful, they were some kind of attempt to articulate my feelings about writing, which is what this interview is about. The poem came out of a lot of thinking I had been doing about Orpheus, because I had been working on translations of Rilke's *Sonnets to Orpheus* for a long time. So it came directly out of Rilke's idea that the best way to station yourself, not just as an artist, but as a human generally, is in two realms. Rilke uses Orpheus as a figure to unite the two: someone who went down to the under-world and broke bread with the shades and then came back to the world again.

It is back to the whole thing that as humans you are in a unique position of having foreknowledge of your own death, which gives you a different perspective from every other mammal. Rilke's idea is that this gives humans a kind of stereoscopic view of the world, one of which is almost as a ghost, and the other as a living being, and that between the two, you find a true place for yourself that resolves all those paradoxes of why we are here, which tend to dog us. That idea is central to any writing of poetry, *I* think: to seek some kind of resolution to those things which can be contradictory.

I think 'The Landing' strikes a balance between the upbeat and the downbeat. I find it much harder to write poems that are celebratory – I think that is just a temperamental disability of mine. Although a lot of poets have a saying that 'happiness writes white', meaning that when you are in love, and really want to write about it, it is like trying to do it in Tippex. But once you are in the purgatorial, there is much more shadow and shade and more complex relationships, which are easier to write about, so I think I am attracted to that kind of subject matter.

In this particular poem I have used straight ballad metre, but made it slightly harder for myself than usual in that both pairs of lines are rhymed. Form is terribly important to me – beyond importance. It is inconceivable that I wouldn't be thinking about form when I was writing a poem. A poem is going to have a form anyway, and not to take care of it seems derelict, really. Also if there is no play, no resistance, then there is no point in doing it, because there is no *game*, no fun in it. It would just be as though you were trying to get the thing written as quickly as possible.

For me, the whole point is the process. And in order to create a process, you almost have to put interesting obstacles in your path, against which you are going to throw this material, this poem, that you think you want to write. Between the play of the two you end up with something entirely different from the poem you suspected you were going to write. If there was no form you could just write what you thought, which would probably be what you already knew, and it would surprise no one. If you don't surprise yourself, the whole enterprise is a waste of time as far as I am concerned.

Because we are all the same, if the subject of a poem is something you already know, the chances are other people will know it too. Or even if it is something others don't know, if I know it, I would be putting it in such a way that I am bored and familiar with, having told myself this story so many times in my head. So there has to be a surprise either in the way you tell things, or in the thing itself. You hope that the whole process that you have been through in writing the poem will be mirrored in the reader's experience in reading it. Without that journey, there can be no possible revelation on their part, so it is part of the contract.

Often the things which resist any kind of articulation are exactly the things you tend to try to be writing about in a poem. So I think you have to find devious means to approach them, which is where obliquity comes in. Very often you are working at the very edge of language and what it can do. All the words you have don't seem to be sufficient for the task, so you are trying to recombine them in strange and interesting ways to extend the range and number of possibilities they might have. That is where *metaphor* comes in: throwing unusual combinations of things together to create a third thing that didn't exist in the language before. That is what excites me about poetry. But of course that whole area is one of *failure*. I think that most poets' experience of writing is one of failure most of the time because you are trying to do something that the language isn't really built for.

But it is the *process* that makes you go on trying. I think it takes you a long time to discover that as a poet. You think that you will get the kick out of getting a book published and being pleased with yourself and getting a good review or whatever. And of course, when that happens, it is lovely and you are grateful for it, don't get me wrong, but there is often that hint of post-Christmas let-down about it: it is not what you thought it was going to be. And that makes you realize what was really exciting about it; and that is *writing* the thing. If the only true engagement you have with poetry is in writing it, then why make the process quick? The whole point is the discoveries you have on the road, and it is that journey which is the most satisfying thing, for me, anyway.

I see the whole composition process as one which starts with inspiration and goes through various stages which might be more, or less, interesting, and ends with publication. Publication is the end of the relationship for me really. You love something, like a child that grows up in your house, but then you have to let it go. To go on pretending that you are going to go on being the poem's child-bearer/apologist is just nuts. You have to let it make its own way in the world and also you need to move on and write something different, or you end up trapped in a cycle of self-impersonation.

That is my main misgiving about public readings. They forge much too close a relationship between you and the work, which is false. Sometimes, it can appear proprietorial, and the whole point is that you are trying to give the stuff away. You are trying to make something so beautiful that somebody wants it for themselves. But when you do a reading, very often the gesture appears to be, 'This is me. I am giving of myself. This is my work', and that is not necessarily how you feel at all! It is always worrying to me when folk come up afterwards and say, 'It is really good to hear the poems read in your voice; I'll know how to read them now.' And you think, 'That's a nice thing to say, but I want you to read them in *your* voice.'

I still don't really like to be called a 'poet'. I think you are only a poet when you are writing a poem. Poetry describes an act, not necessarily a permanent disposition. I mean if you think of yourself as a poet, what kind of behaviour does it entail? Maybe it is the same as calling yourself a plumber. I am not so sure about it

any more, to be honest. But it seems to me that poetry is different from plumbing in that poetry, at the end of the day, has to be
an amateur pursuit, in the best possible sense. I don't think you
can do just that and nothing else for a living. I don't think you
can sit down every day and write a poem, nor should you try to.

I have had really long gaps between books when poetry
retreats to the furthest corner of the universe. For instance poetry
is the last thing on my mind at the moment. I couldn't write a
poem now to save myself. Although I did make one up the other
day, which was a good exercise, because a friend of mine was
getting married and he wanted me to write something, so that
was fun. I feel more part of the community here than I have in
places before. I like the idea that you could actually write something that was of use to someone – that was a new one to me. So
I thought I would have a crack, so I did that poem. But it isn't a
calling for me. I am writing at the moment – but other stuff. I am
doing some translation and some prose. I have got a book of
aphorisms coming out next month.

I don't write longhand at all: I am fully computerized and
I have been for years. But I am mad for new technology – I love
it. So rather shamefully, most of the writing gets done on a tiny
little Psion palm-top, because it fits in my back pocket and I can
do it in the car or in the bus or whatever. I always think of myself
as transferring these poems onto the big screen at the end of the
day and doing some serious work on them, but most of them get
finished on that machine. I remember John Burnside being
appalled when he saw me typing away on this wee thing,
because he likes to feel the flow of the ink through the pen, and
a lot of writers are like that. But you can 'fetishize' technology
just the same way as people who have beautiful stationery and
lovely pens.

I find the winter good for writing, but summer is the only
bad time, I think. There are always great weird things happening in spring and autumn at the change in seasons. Most people

probably find themselves open to strange things then. I used not to mind what time of day I wrote, but now, with all these kids kicking about, it is when they are asleep. So it is in the morning and very late at night, but that will change.

I have a lovely study here at home, which is great and all set up for writing, but so often I just find myself staring out of the window, which is the condition of the writer, I know. To be honest I find it much more productive going out and getting on a train and going into a café. Again it is almost like that resistance thing. If there is something to resist, like noise to shut off, it helps me build a wee space in my head that I can go into – whereas it is quite hard to build that space in silence sometimes.

I started writing in earnest when I was 21. I am a great believer in these things being wound up and ready to go, but it just takes the right combination of circumstances to get them triggered. I left school early, but to be a musician, not to be stupid. I left to play my guitar, which is what I did. There may have been a few wee angst-driven poems in my teens about infinity and sexual frustration: the sort of thing you write about when you are 15. But the occasion came up when I was 21 because I had something to say – to a girl. It wouldn't have happened if I hadn't heard Tony Harrison on the TV one night in a bedsit in Tottenham, which totally blew me away. It switched something on in my head and I 'got it' and kind of understood what it was I wanted to try to do.

So I read his book and everyone else's I could get, and made a really big study of it. Then the occasion came up when I had something to say and I decided I wanted to write a long verse letter so I did it in rhymed tetrameter couplets. I did it until three o'clock in the morning for three months, getting the thing right. It was just part of serving my apprenticeship but I didn't really understand that at the time. And then some time later I had my first book published – a young man's book – I think I have become more sober.

I used to worry who I was writing for, and the internal reader and all that, but I have learnt not to. You do have a kind of internal reader as editor, but if you worry about an audience you start getting into that awful thing about second-guessing what people might like and what they might *get* and understand and you can't do that. When you are over the kind of red-eyed, wild, inspirational bit at the start, which doesn't last for very long, you need to find something between that and a colder, much bluer eye. I always think about that two eyes thing.

The process is always different from poem to poem and you have to learn to keep it flexible. But if you were to characterize it, you have that bit at the start when you get something for nothing: the inspiration that comes with the force of a miracle. It works because it is two things you have never thought of putting together before. Whether it is two words, or two ideas, or an image. It is to do with synthesizing those two things. That synthesis is the process and you need to understand it to find the form of your poem. So first you get a few lines that come very quickly. Then within those lines, I try to divine the form, because there is always something within them which suggests it in terms of its narrative or argumentative shape, or in terms of its metre or rhyme scheme. That is when you get it out of your head and start getting it onto the paper.

I don't want the reader to be aware of the metre or rhyme scheme – they are the means by which you weave the spell, but it should always look easy. On the other hand, if the whole poem really comes easily, I would be almost certain that it was no good. Gradually the distance between you and the poem grows and grows until you can finally let it go out of the house to publication. I see the relationship between me and the poem widening as it goes on. Then I get more of an idea about how other people are going to read it, or how I would read it if I came across it in a book. You are finally able to leap outside the poem and read it as if it was someone else's poem.

On average this process takes about a year for each poem, but I would be working on more than one at a time. You are making sure each word is the right one, but also sometimes striking out whole stanzas that don't belong there. Often if I get the form right, I know I can finish the poem. If I don't understand what the form is, that means I don't understand the poem and the shape of it. It can take as much as three years, but at least then I know I can finish it. I make it sound like a very deliberate thing, but it is not. It is so instinctive. And the instinct gets better calibrated as you go along. And more and more you get a green light saying this is absolutely the way to go with this. But sometimes you just don't get that green light and there are quite a lot of things that have just ended up in the bin, because I have never managed to work out the *shape* of them.

On a conscious level the craft is more important than the subject. The point of keeping the form at the front is so your unconscious can work properly. Otherwise, although this might sound crazy, you can attend consciously to your unconscious which is a disaster. You need to give that conscious part of your brain something to chew on. You know that you are on to something, if while going through this process, you are scared and euphoric. If you don't get that excitement at the start, for me, it is probably a test that you probably don't have a real poem. That is the point. That fear and wonder is *exactly* the feeling that you want the reader to have. I do believe it has to be totally mirrored in you.

I used to dismiss it when people said my poetry was influenced by the fact that I'm a musician, but I don't know any more. If you have two skeletons in the same body they cannot help but be in dialogue with each other and inform one another by analogy. There are quite a few things about poetry and music which are quite close, but a lot of them are false analogies. But there is no doubt that it tunes your ear and helps you listen to a language in different ways if you are a musician.

Very often I find myself quite unconsciously trying to make one big word out of every line – maybe using several words with similar sounds – in the same way that you cannot have all the colours of the rainbow in one tiny bit of a painting. It is instinctive, but you try to limit the vowel and consonantal power of every line because you know if you make the sounds similar it will make sense. Always. Because the sound and the sense in poetry are the same thing. That is what makes poetry different from any other kind of writing. One minute your ear is leading your brain, the next your brain is leading your ear and these things are completely synthesized in poetry and in music. That is the main analogy – sound and meaning are the same in music, as are form and content.

In the past, if I were stuck for a word in a poem, I would just fill in the stress pattern using purely musical criteria. Then I would tend to look at the sounds in the words on either side of the missing one, and just make up something that probably wasn't a real word. Nine times out of ten an actual word, but very near to that, will end up as the solution. I used to do that deliberately, but now, having done it so often, it happens as a matter of course: it is the way I write.

I worry about repeating myself in poetry and I don't think poets have one voice, but many, and they should use as many as they can comfortably inhabit. The autobiographical content of a poem is often just a tone. One might use the first person in a poem, which is sometimes me and sometimes not. It is a strategy a lot of people use and has to be totally flexible according to what kind of poem you are writing. Sometimes the 'I' is you, because for whatever reason, you are writing more directly of your own experience – but it is always a spectrum. Your own experience is always the starting point.

You also naturally, honestly reflect your environment. But you have an imaginary environment that I think you can change. In the same way that if you are in a relationship which is going badly, you just get one reflection of yourself, apart from the other person all the time: it becomes how you think about yourself. Sometimes people get a terrible negative feedback loop about their own writing and what they see as their influences and it gets into a horrible cycle of self-impersonation. So I feel you look for ways to break you out of that – or you will end up keeping on writing the same poem but worse.

One of the ways I like to try to do this is by writing translations or versions of other poets. Very often you find that when you take on their clothes they fit you just as well as what you thought of as your own. It makes you realize you are reprogrammable. I also sometimes write plays – but only for local audiences from Dundee – I have no aspirations to write for the West End. I don't know whether being from Scotland is important. There were a few poems in Scots in the last book – the first time I've really tried to write seriously in Scots, and it did feel like a forlorn romantic republican gesture, because even Scots don't really understand that stuff. But I suppose I did it because one of the nice things about having even urban Scots is that it affords you an intimate register, denied to the middle classes!

It is ridiculous, because I am middle class myself. But nonetheless growing up with that register of speech did give you an intimacy of address that I really miss and would like to keep. But the trouble with these sorts of intimate address is that they are exclusive registers, so I am very wary of using them, because they cut a lot of people out. The thing is probably not to be too self-conscious about it – or you would not use classical references either. You cannot second-guess what people will understand, and once you go down that road you wouldn't know where to stop. The only thing to do is to occasionally have that 'blue eye' I mentioned earlier while you are writing the poem, and stand back and say, 'If I were to read this, would I understand what was being said here?' That is the only test you can have. Anything else is really patronizing. Sometimes you put some reference in which is very obscure, but you can avoid that fairly easily. The only reason for doing it really is to show off, which is daft.

One thing I do write about, perhaps because it is so difficult to talk about, is 'What is the spirit in the modern age?' A lot of the writing which interests me spiritually is from the East. I think there are very few Western authors who have managed to accommodate these ideas in language. If you are writing in Sanskrit, where you have 150 different words for the absolute, and compare that with English that has one, then you have a real problem. So I think poetry inevitably ends up being the surreptitious means by which you attempt to accommodate these ideas in English, or French, or Spanish, or whatever, and some writers do that better than others, but it is very difficult.

I am always most pleased with the last poem I wrote. But the book I like the best is the Antonio Machado, the wee book called *The Eyes*, which is translations of the Spanish poet, because there is less of me in it than the others. I am not trying to say the others are all tainted by self. But there is a kind of transparency – because it was so unlike my own experience – that I like, and that I would like to try to get in my own work. But you can't just decide you would like to do that; you have to work your way towards it. I'd like to think I was doing that.

Winning awards has made it much harder. I mean I am *incredibly* grateful. It is mainly terrific for the book, and you have to keep remembering that it is the book which is getting the prize, not you. You are just as much of a schmuck as you were yesterday, before you got the prize, but the book will do better as a result. So that is the really gratifying thing – it is nice to think of the book doing well. The other scary thing is that expectations are built up when you have won something. But that *should* be the scary thing for everyone. If someone tells you they like your work, you don't want to disappoint them by writing something bad.

But of course being Scottish, all the prize ever does is to send you into a kind of spiral of self-loathing, so it doesn't do you any good at all. I mean the money is great, don't get me wrong. But it is really a Calvinist thing, which says, 'You are no good and you will never be any good', which gets you up every morning. Self-loathing gets me out of bed! Scots Calvinists aren't very good at crediting themselves with anything. But that is not such a bad thing.

Poetry is really the best game, but it isn't fun. Although of course fun for a Calvinist does not imply joy. But if there is no play, what is the point? I am aiming for a kind of transparency that I will probably never achieve, but which I see in the work of those writers that I admire the most. I don't know if I will manage it, but I would like to get there. Occasionally you write the odd line that has a sniff of the weightlessness of the pure lyric. But I'm not sure if I'll get there, you know.

# Willy Russell

*Willy Russell writes plays, musicals and songs, and has recently written a novel. But when he writes a musical he writes both lyrics and score, and when a play of his is turned into a screenplay, it is he who writes that too. Born near Liverpool in 1947, he spent his early years 'sagging' off school to go to the Cavern at the time when the Beatles were playing. Willy Russell left school with one O-level in English. His father worked in a factory, and later ran a fish and chip shop; his mother worked in a warehouse. Russell loved reading and had an idea he wanted to be a writer, but did not know how to go about it. At his mother's suggestion he became a women's hairdresser, writing songs and a bit of poetry in his spare time. At 20, he decided he wanted to go to college, and worked in the Ford car factory cleaning girders to raise money for the fees. He became a teacher, started going to the theatre and began to write plays.*

*In 1992 Liverpool University made Willy Russell a Doctor of Literature. He has won countless prizes including ones for Best Musical and Best Comedy, as well as Bafta, Olivier and Tony awards. He is particularly good at portraying women, working-class struggles and a sense of hope in bleak circumstances. Twenty years after it opened in 1983,* Blood Brothers *is still playing in London's West End, while* Educating Rita *is studied as a GCSE text. With all his success, I was not surprised that the letter I received from him saying that he would be happy to be interviewed was written on his company headed paper, W. R. Limited.*

*I first met Willy Russell when I was working as an assistant stage manager at Liverpool Playhouse in 1980–1. This meant I was in the exciting position of helping out with a production of* One For the Road, *which was still having rewrites as it was being rehearsed. I remember the ending was not finalized till the last moment, which certainly kept us on our toes. Also, unusually, Willy invited all the actors and backstage staff out for a drink one evening. A few months later I was able to watch William Gaunt and Kate Fitzgerald in* Educating Rita *in a production directed by Willy Russell. He was not as well known then as now, but I think we all felt privileged to work with him.*

## Select Bibliography

Plays
*Sam O'Shanker* (1972), *Stags and Hens* (1978), *Educating Rita* (1985), *Shirley Valentine* (1988)

Musicals
*John, Paul, George, Ringo . . . and Bert* (1974), *Blood Brothers* (1983)

TV
*Our Day Out* (1976), *Terraces* (1993)

Films
*Educating Rita* (1983), *Shirley Valentine* (1989)

Novel
*Wrong Boy* (2000)

Album
*Hoovering the Moon* (2004)

From *Educating Rita* (Act One, scene 7):

> RITA (*angrily*): I didn't want to come to your house just to play the court jester.
> FRANK: You weren't being asked to play that role. I just – just wanted you to be yourself . . .

RITA: I'm all right with you, here in this room; but when I saw those people you were with I couldn't come in. I would have seized up. Because I'm a freak. I can't talk to the people I live with any more. An' I can't talk to the likes of them on Saturday, or them out there, because I can't learn the language. I'm a half-caste. I went back to the pub where Denny was, an' me mother, an' our Sandra, an' her mates. I'd decided I wasn't comin' here again. . . . Just because you pass a pub doorway an' hear the singin' you think we're all OK, that we're all survivin', with the spirit intact. Well I did join in with the singin', I didn't ask any questions, I just went along with it. But when I looked round me mother had stopped singin', an' she was cryin', but no one could get it out of her why she was cryin'. Everyone just said she was pissed an' we should get her home. So we did, an' on the way I asked her why. I said, 'Why are y' cryin', Mother?' She said, 'Because – because we could sing better songs than those.' Ten minutes later, Denny had her laughing and singing again, pretending she hadn't said it. But she had. And that's why I came back. And that's why I'm staying.

*       *       *

This may sound flippant, but it is not: I start with the deadline. If there is no deadline, I will never write anything. I write because I *have* to write because I have usually entered into a contract. I will always try to get out of that contract. In monetary terms, I can do that, but if I am locked into a contract that I *morally* can't get out of, then I will have to write the play. Now that was the case with *Educating Rita*. I tried to get out of it a few times. I was trying to write *a* play – I had no idea what, and the deadline was looming.

By the time I was commissioned to write *Educating Rita* I had already had a big West End success with my play about the

Beatles. I had had quite a number of TV pieces broadcast and had also written a play called *Breezeblock Park*. That had a rather chequered history, but Walter Donohue, the literary manager at the Royal Shakespeare Company, had seen it when it was in London. It was seeing that play which made him want to commission me to write a play for the Warehouse, which was at that time the RSC's experimental London home.

I didn't think I would be able to come up with anything for the Warehouse, so I called Walter Donohue, and tried to persuade him to do something which would happen later – a musical version of my TV film *Our Day Out* – which I thought was a brilliant idea. He thought it was a good idea too, but at that time, 99 per cent of the RSC's resources were committed to doing the David Edgar version of *Nicholas Nickleby*, so they couldn't take on that kind of a project. So I had to go back to the desk because I was morally committed, and carry on the *miserable* existence of looking at very long days in which I would write, but nothing would ignite, or become fertilized.

In that process, at some point, Rita walked onto the page intact, with the voice. And the voice was everything. It always is with me, the *voice* is where it will begin. And, for me, it is an exciting voice, and one that I know I will be able to say all kinds of things in, but it has to thrill me. On a simple level, I can recreate that voice in my head and I know that the sound of it and what it is saying will be theatrically dynamic. For instance, the whole of the first scene of *Educating Rita* is about *voice*. It is about two voices – two foreign languages – colliding, testing, juxtaposing and counterpointing.

In the lines I chose to quote, towards the end of the first act, in retrospect, one could attribute to oneself a certain consciousness and motive that in fact probably wasn't there at the time. If we could go back and be inside my mind at the time I was writing this part of *Educating Rita*, you would probably find I was struggling to find my way through: struggling with the plot apart from anything else. I never start off with a heavily conscious idea of what it is I want to say. That has to emerge as naturally and as gracefully as possible through pursuing both the voices of the character and the plot journey. Once I have got that voice, I know I will finish the play. But I don't know what the hell it will be.

Liverpool is a place that is not afraid of language. I don't think this play would have occurred if I had been a writer from Ashby-de-la-Zouche. But had I been a Glaswegian or a Dubliner or from a place like, say, Bermondsey that has a fiercely proud, and unfortunately sometimes chauvinistic, working-class tradition, then it could have come out of anywhere like that. It would have to come from an urban city environment.

My very first efforts at writing, while I was at college, were a couple of television plays, which didn't work. But when they were rejected the producers at the time, David Rose and Barry Hansom, wrote very detailed letters explaining why they were rejecting – pointing out what was really good in the work and what flawed it. So I learnt an enormous amount from that. I was writing those on spec, but during that period, the second year at St Catherine's College, my year was meant to be doing the major production. We had been told that we were going to do *Peer Gynt*, but for some reason that was abandoned, and instead our year was to present an evening of one-act plays, monologues – a kind of compendium evening.

I went to one of the tutors, Fred Steadman-Jones, and asked, 'Would you do one of my "one-acters"?' and he looked at me rather startled, but said, 'Let me see something, and we'll consider it'. So I walked off rather pleased with myself and then realized I didn't have any one-act plays, and I had to write one in a week to give it to him when I saw him in my next tutorial – so that was a deadline again. Right from the word go, I have had deadlines. I think that for me, and for quite a lot of people I know, if there is no deadline – no external reason for finishing the play – you have always got more time in which to make better this idea.

When you have a deadline you have got to deliver by a particular date, and in a sense, responsibility is to a certain extent taken out of your hands. When you deliver the play you can think, 'Well it is not the best thing that I could ever write, but it is the best thing I could write within that time.'

Once a play has taken off – I've got that voice and I know that something is happening – in the same nanosecond it can be exhilarating and the most depressing experience you can possibly imagine. That is the nature of the beast, and I do it because I *need* to do it. The sense of satisfaction that comes with doing it and getting it *right* is unparalleled. I do not do many drafts of any stage play, although it is always delivered in a very 'playable' state. But once we are in rehearsals, I will rewrite like hell. Prior to word-processing I would first write in longhand and then type up. Next I would meet with the director and take the director's and producer's notes and probably do some small amount of rewriting. Then I would rewrite through the rehearsal period, then open, and *that* is when the rewriting really starts for me! Some things you *cannot* tell until the play is in the place where it really happens – in the theatre with an audience.

Broadly, my favourite genre is theatre. I don't want to upset the novel that I wrote, or films that I've done, but the zenith for me is theatre, because it is a poetic medium. It is a distilled medium, in which you have to engage the imagination of the audience. It is not a literal medium, like film. You can't put everything before the audience. What I love about theatre is solving the problems. With a film camera, it is easy: you can take the eye of the audience to wherever the action is, no matter how minute that action. In theatre you have to constantly find ways of *convincingly* bringing the action before the eye of the audience.

So with *Educating Rita*, for instance, a vast proportion of the action takes place off stage. I had to keep finding ways of bringing that action *on* stage before the audience, and to do it in a way that does not look contrived or improbable. Coping with those restrictions of the unities of time and space, and playing within that crucible, means you are dealing with something 'poetic'. I am not talking about verse drama or high-flown language, but the nature of theatre itself – and that is to distill to its very, very essence, in the way that poetry does.

I did write a lot of original screenplays but they were at a time when they were films for television. When I wrote a film called *One Summer,* I had rather an unfortunate experience with it and took my name from it, but actually I was as proud of that script as I was of *Educating Rita.* It is just that at that time, television as I had known it was changing out of all recognition, and if I was going to be working with back-stabbing bastards in British television, I could get paid a lot more working in Hollywood, where at least they stab you in the chest!

The other things I have written are musicals. Then I would generally write the lyrics first. You have to write a song at a certain point in the show, that achieves something. So the requirements of plot and libretto dictate what the song should be. Then you have to have the music in the most harmonious tonality to the requirements of the piece. In something like *Blood Brothers,* I will sit down and try to construct a lyric, and come up, for example, with a song called 'Easy Terms' which was good because it immediately had a double meaning. Then I will decide a certain melody fits the requirements and is right for that moment. However, in stand-alone songs, 99.9 per cent of the time I will write the music first, and that will largely dictate the nature of the lyric.

I have been lucky in that I have worked with some of the best. Julie Walters is just an astonishing actress. Barbara Dickson is an astonishing singer. She is not the world's greatest actress – and I think she would agree with that, but at the time that I did *John, Paul, George, Ringo . . . and Bert,* back in those days, the English musical was a contradiction in terms. It was dogged by the attitude of the English theatre towards the musical. Any musicals that were written were cast from very good actors and actresses who couldn't sing a bloody note. In West End terms it was accepted that you could just act your way through some of this stuff, and it was often absolutely horrendous.

Because I came initially from a musical background, rather than a theatrical one, I knew what audiences wanted. Whenever I do any piece of work I always imagine the most unforgiving, non-theatre-going audience possible. The audience in my head would never sit through that kind of bad singing. But I *knew* if they heard singing of the calibre of Barbara Dickson, who was then totally unknown, they would completely forgive any inadequacies in acting – but it wouldn't work the other way round. I have to win the audience. No assumptions can be made. You have to go out and win that audience.

People have sometimes said that I am good at depicting women, but hand on heart I haven't got a clue why. True, I was brought up with lots of aunties around, and I was a hairdresser listening to women. With hindsight, I can look back and say it might be this or that, or it might just be that I was rather canny and realized at that time that the theatre world was complaining about the lack of starring roles for actresses rather than actors. It may also be that for me, being a male heterosexual, it is much more sexy to have a woman on stage than a load of guys!

I remember with *Educating Rita*, I could have written a play where the Rita character was a man. But it wouldn't have that sexual *frisson* which is central to the play, even though the play never even mentions it. So maybe it is that kind of theatrical instinct again – what will grab an audience? E. M. Forster called it 'the atavistic worm of wanting to know what happens next'. It is plot again, and you can't have any story without that.

I am probably most proud of something which doesn't yet exist. That is not to say that I am not proud of what I have done, but I can't separate one title from another, because if you do, the others get jealous. I do think of them like that. The writer's books or plays as children is a very good, but over-worked analogy, so

I am fighting shy of it. But they *are* like kids and they all have different characteristics. I used to be ambitious, and I am still fiercely ambitious for my work, but whether I am still as ambitious for myself, I don't know. In many ways I have fulfilled a lot of that fierce ambition I had. My biggest ambition, I think, was to get myself out of a life situation in which people for whom I had no respect, and who deserved no respect, had control over me and my life.

So now I do have more control, and a company and everything. People still like to maintain the mythical notion of the rarified artist who does not deal with the earthly facts that the rest of society has to deal with. But that is a *completely* false notion. Shakespeare was an actor, he had a company, he ran the company, he did the books. This business is called show business, and it is a business. If you don't attend to that side of it, the chances are that you won't be able to put shows on.

I haven't felt excited by what has been going on in the theatre for quite some time, which is perhaps why my most recent work has been the novel and an album. It is not to say that marvellous things have not been happening in the theatre, because they have, but the whole *regional* theatre movement that I was really kind of a part of, was decimated in the Thatcherite years, and it has still not really recovered from that. So there is nowhere particularly now that I can look at and say, 'I would love to be involved there.' There is no central theatrical home for me that I see screaming out at the moment.

When I think about writing a stage play, and I *have* been thinking about it, my instinct at the moment is to assemble my own company, and find my own space, and do it that way. That is not because I want to control everything about it – but I would want input. For instance I have just done a show with Tim Firth in Edinburgh, and although my company completely financed that, there were very strong voices around Tim and me. It certainly wasn't a case of everybody coming in and catering to *my* ego.

But then again, I may not be writing a play because I have always dreaded the blank page. The latest thing I have written is an album of songs, and I enjoyed that *enormously*. It was recorded over a very leisurely period, and it didn't have a deadline, I have to say! It was a lot of sitting on trains writing lyrics, and sitting in studios with guitars and keyboards, and it was a very different, happy experience for me. Writing plays, on the other hand, you are diving off a very high board and you don't even know if there is any water in the pool below you! You just hope that you get wings before you hit the concrete.

# Graham Swift

*Graham Swift comes across as gentle, quiet and passionate about his work: an unusual combination, which is reflected in his novels. His books work on many levels, and are stories of people written about with affection and poignancy as well as superlative craft and narrative skill. In virtually all his books strands of subplot, different voices and internal monologues interweave; language is both economic and lyric; and themes recur. But each novel is very different, and surprisingly, none draws directly on personal experiences: Swift is a champion of the imagination.*

*Graham Swift has been called 'one of our finest novelists'. He was born in 1949 and attended Cambridge and then York University. Until the success of* Waterland *(described by the* Observer *as a 'masterpiece') he taught English part time. To date he has written one book of short stories and seven novels. His work has been translated into 25 languages and won many awards, including the Booker Prize for* Last Orders.

## Selected Bibliography

Short Stories
*Learning to Swim and Other Stories* (1982)

Novels
*The Sweet Shop Owner* (1980), *Waterland* (1983), *Ever After* (1991), *Last Orders* (1996), *The Light of Day* (2003)

The following extract is from the end of *The Light of Day*: George, an ex-policeman turned private investigator, imagines the day when his client, Sarah, with whom he has fallen in love, will be released from prison. Play on words, repetition and resonance give the passage its poetic quality:

> Fog. Everything hidden and lost. Would that be right? To slip back into the world when it's only half there. Secretly and undercover at first – the full thing might be too much. Like prisoners who step the other way under a blanket, as if they're naked, through the last stab of light.
>
> A blanket of fog. Here, have this blanket. All the blankets.
>
> A foggy day, everything wrapped in grey.
>
> No. I want it to be like this day, that's already slipped into night. A hard night coming, you can tell already, another hard frost. But tomorrow will be like today, brilliant, blue and still.
>
> I want it to be like today. When I'm there, when I'm waiting, heart thudding, my breath billowing before my eyes, when she comes back, steps out at last into the clear light of day.

*        *        *

I write with a fountain pen and black ink. My fountain pens are very precious to me and I would never take them out of the house. I have written three novels with my current pen and all the others were written with another fountain pen, which died, but I still have it. I am very much a hand-writer. I have a computer, and in the last stages of a novel I use it, and indeed, find it very valuable, to do all those editing things which used to be incredibly time-consuming on a typewriter. But I would only go to it at that late stage. The actual creative work of composition is always with pen and ink. I just don't think, for me, it could be otherwise, because I think very strongly that a pen gets

whatever is in your head on to the page more quickly and efficiently than anything that has been invented. Computer people
would dispute that, and my handwriting is virtually illegible,
even for me, but when I write, I do any number of squiggles and
little signs, which are messages to me about things, and I could
only do them with a pen.

I have a room at the back of the house where I write. I am not
a systematic note-taker, or planner, but I do jot things down if a
thought comes to me, before I forget it, on anything available,
like the back of a bus ticket. I don't have a nice notebook, but
masses of bits of paper with odd scraps of information, which
may, or may not, go into the final mix. I scarcely think about it
now, in that it is so routine that I pick up a pen and scrawl, if I can,
on a page. But even those routines start with their rituals and
have a sort of magic. I would probably get quite upset to have
the routine taken away. If I didn't have my room, with its
corners, my pen, the ordinary lined notepad that I use, I would
feel a bit lost, for a while at least. I know there are plenty of
writers who can do it anyhow, anywhere, travelling, using a
laptop – I don't understand that, but we are all different.

I would like to be as honest as I can about how I start a book,
but the more honest I am, the more it will seem that I am not
really telling you anything. I have written seven novels and am
writing another now. How they begin really is a mystery to me.
Usually, when I am asked, what I would say, which is half-true,
is that it is always something small. A novel is a very big under-
taking, but I don't have a big idea. Even the phrase 'having an
idea for a novel' is a rather bogus one for me. It grows somehow
mysteriously from some small beginning, which even I can't necessarily remember.

What happens is that you are glad that it is beginning, even if
it proves to be the wrong thing. You are so glad that it has started,
that you don't really care how it began or how it will continue.
I will get to a point where I feel inside that it is brewing. Then

you feel two things in conflict: you just want to get on and write, but you can't afford to do that because you must have some sort of shape. So you look for the framework so you can continue to write, while another part of you knows that you are only going to discover some things by the writing anyway. You are in a weird double-bind and neither guarantees the other. So you are in a crazy situation, but I accept the illogicality of it. I am sure there are many writers who sense there is a novel, and make a plan and then write it, but I can't do that.

My biggest fear all the time is to lose the real inspiration. If you sit and think carefully and systematically about something, my fear is that will cancel out the real emotion. I am guided very strongly by instinct, intuition and feeling, which don't fit into rational schemes. I have found this to be the case the more I have written. On the other hand, I don't think you can separate form and content, and both things are as important as each other to me, and together they make the thing itself. I do care about shape and form and have that real artistic ambition and instinct that I want to make something well-shaped. But I also care about content very much. Novels don't happen to me very often, in that I don't write them easily and quickly, and that is really because strong content doesn't come along very often. So it matters that if I am going to write something which may take me years, I have found the strong content that will propel it.

My working day is very early. I can be at work as early as 5.30 in the morning. That is how it has been for a long time. I need, I relish, I like, I have got into the habit of, this early part of the day, when I have the feeling that the rest of the world is asleep, but I am alert, and am not going to be interrupted. If you get going in those early hours you are launched and safe. The theory is that I work up till midday, and will have done a real day's work, and the rest of the day is open. It seldom goes according to this plan, but that is the idea, and the early morning thing is peculiarly important. It is almost like getting up early to go hunting: the feeling that it *will* happen in these special hours. Often it doesn't, but that is in the nature of writing. Of course if you have had a late night, you are tired, but at best, there is a real excitement. I make myself a pot of coffee and take it up to the room where I work. It is dark outside, everything is quiet and I feel a nice, intense, concentrated feeling and I get on – I don't think I could do that if I started work at nine or ten in the morning.

I do a hell of a lot of rewriting, both as I write and at later stages, so a book tends to take around three years or longer – more if you take into account the first notion to when you have the final manuscript. And sometimes I don't just rewrite; I reject and start again. My finished books are not in straight chronological sequence – anyone reading any one of my novels would see straight away that I move around in time – but I move around in time as I write. I make some decisions afterwards about rearranging the order here or there, but I would more or less write it in the order in which the reader reads it, embracing all the leaps in time as I go along. For example, in *Last Orders*, you are jumping in time and from one character to another, and conceivably someone could take it all apart and wonder if I might have had a completely different structure at first, where I followed one character all the way through. But no, I somehow knew when it should be Ray, or Vince, and when it should be in the present or the past. I had an intuition about it and that is very much how I write.

It is a natural habitat for me, and one that we all exist in, because I think it is the habitat of memory. Memory is not sequential. We are all formed by our past, and even as we walk about in the present, we are the creatures of time. I have always written in the first person, and one thing that does is to give you access to a character's memory as it exercises itself. That would be a much more laborious thing to do in the third person, where you would constantly have to flag it, saying something like, 'As X walked along the street he was remembering that time . . .' which is all rather tedious and stagey, whereas I can just go directly to it.

Men tend to predominate in my books, and in one way you could say that is not so surprising because I am a man, so I would feel comfortable and sure writing from a male point of view. On the other hand, I don't really see it as necessarily such a big divide. The big challenge in writing is to write a character. To get from yourself to this other being, and whether they are male or female, is, in a way, secondary. I am writing something now which could work out as about 50 per cent male and 50 per cent female. I have found the way that I do it is not to think male or female. When they are delivering their inner thoughts, are they actually so different? I think it would be a great mistake for a male writer writing a female character, or the other way round, to be constantly tapping themselves on the shoulder and saying, 'Remember you are writing a woman here. Now what would a woman think?' That would be false and artificial and wrongly emphasized.

In a sense, there is no point in writing a novel unless you are communicating and someone is going to read it, but I don't think about that at the time. I just have immense faith and trust that a reader will be there. But the reader is not this person who is inspecting what I do as I write, and saying, 'No, you should do it a different way, or it won't satisfy me.' I just go by intuition and I don't think I am very different from the reader. I happen to be the writer, and I happen to have some talent, but I am just another human being.

When I have talked about writing in the past, I have possibly over-stressed the fact that my own life, my biography, is not the stuff of my fiction. I have said things like, 'One writes fiction because one doesn't want to write fact', and I do feel that you need to keep your subject matter at a distance from you, so that your imagination can take flight to it. That's what's exciting; getting from what you know into what you don't know. I really do have a tremendous faith in writing as a leap into the unknown. But it is a leap that you take with the sort of rope of the imagination to hang on to.

Some novelists, particularly in their early work, write fairly autobiographically, and are taught to write what they know, and there is a logic to that. But my first novel, apart from its south London location, was not autobiographical. I frequently write about parents and children – being responsible for another generation – but I don't have children, although I obviously had parents. I would say that my early family life was quite happy and secure, which wouldn't be true of many of the families I have written about. Also, people tend to assume that because I have written about the Fenland, where I never lived, or eels, or the French Revolution, that I do a great deal of research. In fact I don't, I find that all rather tedious, and try to get away with the minimum.

A thing that really does interest me, and is a real area of my work, is the question of should this thing be told or not? Maybe that is partly because as a novelist, I am a teller. So I am always making decisions about what should be told at this point or later – but that is fairly technical. I am more fascinated with how, in life, we all come up against knowledge, which may or may not be shared or imparted, and how knowledge is both an enlightening thing, but also sometimes dangerous and destructive. Secrets fascinate me. We are embedded in secrets, in that none of us knows the whole story about where we are in relation to other people. I think I will always write about that.

Sometimes I have taken it to a sort of intellectual pitch. For instance, I wrote a novel called *Ever After*, where there was a certain amount of stuff about the Darwinian moment in the nineteenth century, when this bit of scientific knowledge, virtually held by this one man, was released into the world. That was scientific truth, but it also upset a great many people's understanding of the world they lived in. But this sort of thing happens in much more intimate ways in personal life. It is something which is curiously important to me and is a feature of my work that despite myself, I keep coming back to.

My instinct goes against the advice that writers are often given, which is 'show, don't tell'. In many cases you *should* show rather than tell, if that effectively means show rather than *explain*. But the word 'tell' is a great word. It means more than just the simple 'I am now telling you this thing.' We use it in so many ways: '*I* can tell' means something quite different from the business of saying something; it means knowing and understanding, and I feel that these two senses are involved. So there are times when what you have to do is not show, which would be almost the easy thing, but find a way of telling.

There are times in writing, which are a little like the times in life when you say to someone who may be very close, and it may be a very painful thing, 'I've got to tell you something.' It is not a question of showing, but of finding a way inside you of how it would be best to impart what you have to impart. Finding the way to tell things goes with being human. That situation isn't about storytelling, but any narrative brings out in you your ability to shape something so that it will communicate without it being a simple matter of explaining or informing; it will give something more than that. And of course part of telling is not telling, and that is the same with writing. It may sound a contradiction, but you can often better tell something by not telling it. I am very aware that you must leave spaces for the reader's mind to use.

Storytelling is a primitive thing going back long before books. People have a need to tell and hear stories; it is human nature. But we live more and more in a world where we pretend we don't need that – where it may be considered a bit naïve and sentimental, compared to the culture of information. So I think, sadly, the novel needs to hold its own more and more against that sea of stuff around it. But I think it will always hold its own because although it is a sophisticated literary form, it is storytelling, and people will always turn to it. And in the end, I am a storyteller, using the novel, which is a wonderful, all-embracing, elastic form. I do also have a kind of musical sense of storytelling and how a novel is structured. I will feel it needs to move in a certain way and have that rhythm and echo, before I have necessarily found the right words.

I taught myself to write – I didn't have any mentor or teacher. I think I became an apprentice writer in my early 20s, but I had wanted for some time before then to be a writer. I grew up in the 50s when the book, or the word, was what you did for entertainment. I read a lot and I listened to the radio, so I was very word-cultured. There was a time when I thought, how nice it would be to be one of these people who made books and created these wonderful worlds, which opened up as you opened the page. My thoughts were very crude and naïve, but exciting. I wanted to do this magic stuff that writers did. I would find it absolutely charming now, to be presented again with those books that I read when I was eight or nine, because I have forgotten what they were. I would have got them from the library, and to pick them up again would take me back to the germ of it all.

At that time it was not literary ambition, it was just wanting to write books. As I got older, I do remember reading people like Rosemary Sutcliffe, who wrote historical novels, which I would get lost in. But I do know that even at that early age I was able to look at a paragraph and say to myself, 'Gosh, that bit of description is wonderful. How do you do that? If only I could do that!' I can remember having feelings like that which evolved into a desire to be a writer – a bit like wanting to be an engine driver. It never went away and started to move towards a serious intent to be a writer. All the way through my teens, I nursed this, without really owning up to it. Then I went to university at Cambridge and other things got in the way, but when I left, I sort of got myself by the lapel and said, 'Well, are you serious about it? Are you really going to be a writer, because if you are, you must start to write properly.'

So I did. It was by virtue of getting a grant to do a post-graduate course at York University, where I existed under false pretences, because I should have been writing a PhD thesis, but in fact, I was learning to write. During three years I wrote short stories, over and over again. I threw most of them away, and didn't show them to anybody, but nursed an ever-more crystallizing ambition to be a writer. I think when I emerged from those three years, I knew that whatever happened, it was what I was: I was a writer. Even at that point, I was very unsure whether I had any real talent, whether I had a gift. Now I think I do, but then I was not so sure, though I knew I would stubbornly persist.

I carried on writing short stories, feeling that I was a story writer, not a novelist. I then got confident enough to send them to magazines. Rejection slips. I sent several to *London Magazine*, where the editor, Alan Ross, who is no longer alive, alas, was very encouraging, even when he sent me rejection slips. He would write something on the slip, like, 'nearly', and I can't tell you how much those 'nearlys' meant! I felt I had this kind of strange patron, and eventually, he did take a story, and then published others, and I met him. He was one of the most important people in my career.

I vividly remember going to have lunch with him. This was my first real encounter with a person, a writer himself, a poet, from the world of literature. I felt I had, for a moment at least, come out of the cold. There was a point when he said to me – he must have had second-sight – 'I think you might be writing something longer.' I don't know how he knew it, but I was, because I was struggling with what I realize was my first novel, *The Sweet Shop Owner*. He said, 'If you want to show me anything, if you want to show me *it*, if, and when, you finish, I would be interested.' He used to have a small book-publishing outfit, and I showed it to him, around 1976, and two weeks later he said, 'I think it's terrific and I'd like to publish it!'

Of course it was too good to be true, because his publishing business suddenly ran out of money and folded, so he couldn't do it, but he said he would help me to find another publisher. He did, but it took four years, which was a long time to wait, but I think that is how it is: it is a slow and difficult process.

Winning prizes hasn't really made a difference. Of course it enhances your profile and so on, but it doesn't make a difference to me as I am inside, or to the me who sits and writes in this room – that doesn't change. That is the extraordinarily mysterious, and difficult, and sometimes wonderful process that it is, and nothing from the outside will change that.

The same is fundamentally true with regards to the films that have been made of my books. Both the films of *Waterland* and *Last Orders* were good experiences for me, where I got friendly with the directors while they were making the films and they were happy for me to be around. I enjoyed it. Of course it is a wonderful change from the solitary, sometimes lonely business of writing, to go and mix with this great army of people making a film. It is sometimes rather slow and repetitious on a film set, but when they are making a film of your work, it never gets totally boring, because you have to say to yourself, 'Wow! They are doing all this because once I did sit in a chair in that solitary room, and it has caused all this to happen.' You can't resist a childish delight. It is like dressing up with a box of costumes. Certain scenes for *Last Orders* were shot in Balham, just down the road from where I live, and I would go along and see a whole section of Balham High Street turned into a bit of my novel. You would have to be an idiot if you didn't find that rather wonderful, although that is not what it is all about.

I am, unquestionably, proud of every book I've written. If I wasn't, I wouldn't want them to be seen by anyone else. With *Last Orders*, something happened which made the language different. I think it was to do with trusting, more than I ever had done, so-called ordinary language – the language of people who you could say, wrongly, aren't so articulate. I was using a sort of language of the street; not directly, in that it was not like a tape-recording, but I was using it, and found it very liberating. I found all the apparent limitations of it not to be limitations at all, and this language could be very eloquent, just as more articulate language can be a barrier. So I got interested in simpler words, simpler phrases, shorter and more economic sentences, which might be more transparent and might get you more quickly to the things that matter.

That seemed to continue with *The Light of Day*, but I don't know if it will be a continuing trend or not. I chose the passage at the end of *The Light of Day* for you to quote because it is, at this point, the last thing I wrote that is published. There is something nice about that. And I always intended that the final words of the book should be its title. Another thing I did with this book, as with *Last Orders*, was to structure it on a single day. I don't see myself doing that constantly as a formula either, but it was certainly very helpful as a discipline. In *Last Orders* there is a one-day journey and whatever else is going to happen, and a lot else does, I had to get the characters from London to Margate, so I had to think, 'Well, they should be getting to Chatham about now', or whatever.

In *The Light of Day* George has shorter journeys to make through a certain geography on a certain day. So they both had that discipline, although in both I was also dealing with other levels of time. However, I like the focus of a fairly short, defined period, more than I used to. But I wouldn't like to predict how my writing will go. I am writing a novel at the moment, which is first person and more than one character. Who knows if one day I might produce a third-person novel? It is a thing which I have always felt isn't me, but it might be a good thing if it happened. You have to surprise yourself.

The thing I *can* say is that I am a novelist. It is a long while since I have written short stories: occasionally I have, and I would always be happy to spend some time just doing stories again, but it doesn't happen. One of the pleasures of writing a story is that you start it and very soon it will be finished; it might even be today, which is a tremendous morale-boosting achievement. But I think I have a mindset now, which is of the novel. You know you are there for a long haul, which is quite daunting, but I like the feeling that once you have begun a novel, you have your job. You know that you will get up in the morning, in my case quite early, and you will continue this task, which is there for you to do. And it will be like that for a long while and then it will be finished. I like the feeling of being in something big and continuing. I haven't lost that sense of the magic of storytelling, which I must have had when I read the novels, now forgotten, as a child.

Writing is my life. It is not all of my life, by any means, but it is my life and my work in a way that not so many people can say. People do their jobs, but they wouldn't say, 'This is my life. This is me!' And they wouldn't say either, sadly, in most cases, 'This is also what I love. It is the love of my life.' By doing anything that you fundamentally love to do, you are going to suffer for it too; it is going to be painful at times. Love is like that – it is not just a wonderful thing, it is demanding. But I do what I have always wanted to do. Often on the bad days, I can start to think, 'Am I really loving this?' But I do love it and I hope that I write with love. And on the wonderful days, when it goes like it should go, you know that what you have just written you will never have to change, because it is right. It is more than that. It makes you feel that everything is worthwhile. The possibility on any one day of having that feeling is by itself a perfect reason for doing it. It makes you feel in touch with life, and the world; it makes you know why you are here. At best, it is an incredibly intense contact with being here and being alive.

# Eleanor Updale

*Eleanor Updale started writing books fairly recently, and won both a Smarties and a Blue Peter Prize for her first. It is a young adult novel,* Montmorency: *a compelling historical thriller. Previously Updale studied history at Oxford, and was a producer of current affairs programmes for BBC radio and television. Now in middle age, she is writing a PhD; serving on the Clinical Ethics Committee of Great Ormond Street Hospital; writing a series of* Montmorency *books; and is also wife to the broadcaster James Naughtie and mother of three children.*

Meeting Eleanor Updale I was struck by her warmth and an endearing enthusiasm. She delights in the writing process, and uses history in the same way other writers might use fantasy. In Montmorency, when a petty thief crashes through a skylight while attempting escape in Victorian London, his whole life changes. He is revived, reconstructed and shown off in trips from prison by an ambitious young doctor. At the Scientific Society where his scars are being shown, Montmorency hears about London's new sewage system and gains the idea for his life after release. He will have two identities: Scarper, degenerate servant and elusive burglar, and Montmorency, fashionable, wealthy gentleman.

Stephen Fry praised Montmorency as 'one of the most original, witty and delicious books to have arrived for a very long time . . . macabre, funny, suspenseful and humane . . . a unique and brilliant fable that is set to become an instant classic'. Updale's second book about this flawed hero is an equally action-packed adventure. It includes drug addiction, government spies, and the mystery behind a row of tiny graves on a remote Scottish island. The books evolved in the same way, but it was only after interviewing Eleanor Updale that the dedications in her books became clear: 'For Jim, Andrew, Catherine and Flora – Montmorency's oldest friends.'

**Selected Bibliography**

Children's Novels
*Montmorency* (2003), *Montmorency on the Rocks* (2004), *Montmorency and the Assassins* (2005)

From the opening of *Montmorency*:

> The pain woke him again. Not the constant throb that was so familiar he could hardly remember being without it. This was one of those sharp stabs from the wound along his thigh. Doctor Farcett had dug deep to get through to the shattered bone, and the layers of catgut stitching pulled as the torn flesh struggled to realign itself. After so many interventions by the keen young medic, Montmorency should have been prepared for the agony, but each time the after-effects seemed worse, and the limited pain relief (alcohol, and the occasional treat of an experimental gas) less effective.

*   *   *

I had never heard the term 'young adult fiction' before my book came out, and I got sucked into the publishing industry, which has this category. In a way, I think it is a category that does more harm than good, because it excludes younger and older people from it. I just think of myself as a writer of fiction, to be honest. I thought of my first book as a children's book because it grew out of stories I had written for my children. So I didn't put in gratuitous violence, or sex scenes, and I approached children's publishers. But once out, a lot of adults also read that book and wrote to me about it.

While I am writing, I don't think of a target reader at all. I am the servant and master of the story: I am telling the story and it goes where it needs to. *Montmorency* started off as a bedtime story. My three children are all very close together in age. I used to tell a lot of stories; not just because I liked it, but because I used to be so exhausted at the end of the day, I was too tired to read! I preferred to turn off the light and lie down and make it up. The Montmorency stories started when my children were about four, five and six – quite little. But if you are telling the story, it can be about anything – it doesn't have to be about dippy ducks.

When I first told the story, I was literally making it up as I went along. You can picture the scene: exhausted mother, lying on the bed with children who don't want to go to sleep. I started out with the character of Montmorency in prison, and a slightly different story then, where he found out about the sewers in the prison library – which I changed when I wrote the book. In fact I think when I very first told it, he hadn't been injured, or repaired, and there was no doctor. But it was a story that the children always wanted again, and so I would change and embellish it. So I suppose the book is story-driven.

When I came to write it, I thought it was more fun if he went out into society and picked up information. But right from the start of telling the story, I realized he couldn't steal things and then go and sell them as a thief. So I had to set up this whole structure of the double life, and a third place where he would get changed from one life to another. The double life just came from working out the story in my head. I suppose I must have been slightly influenced by *The Elephant Man* and *Dr Jekyll and Mr Hyde*. I wasn't a great reader as a child, so I hadn't read all the children's classics, but I am sure my view of the Victorian world, even though I have done formal work on it as a historian, is, inevitably, heavily influenced by those black-and-white films that used to be on television on Sunday afternoons when I was little. I don't see how you *can't* be influenced by things like that.

But one thing that really annoys me is if you talk to people about the book, and they say, 'Oh! I see, it's like Jekyll and Hyde', or, 'It's like *The Elephant Man*', and I say, 'No, it isn't.' In fact it is very much *not* like the doctor in *The Elephant Man*. My character came much more out of my contacts with doctors now, and their ethical dilemmas, which are eternal. That aspect might be considered too hefty for kids, but I don't think it is. And the moral dilemmas are not what drive the book. I think the characters have to be so complete, that they've got all the faults of a real person, and if you've got that, you are going to have them do things that throw up ethical problems.

As I have been writing, I have got more and more interested in Dr Farcett. In the second book there is a parallel theme running – and it is perfectly all right if you don't notice it is there – about how you do things based on hunches and instinct, and if they turn out all right everybody thinks you are marvellous, and you are a good person. But you can do things from exactly the same motives and it ends up going horribly wrong, and everybody thinks you're appalling. That runs through the book, but most people probably wouldn't notice, because it is actually just what happens in life. But I would rather that I do all this careful crafting and nobody notices. It is like the crinoline under the dress. It would break my heart to see somebody made to write an essay on 'How did she do that?' – I don't want you to know that it is there.

I am an historian by profession so I am used to ordering events in my mind. I do research, but not into the Victorian period, but into seventeenth-century scientific history. Some of the scientific themes and issues which come out of the work I do for a living have found their way into my books, but transposed to the nineteenth century. The third book, which doesn't come out until next year, is even more based in real events than the first two, and so the time structure, although it is a work of fiction, is actually real. There are several real events which happen which my characters get involved in. By the third book, I have established the characters, and so it is much easier for me to play with them, whereas in the first one, I am still introducing them as people. But I never thought, 'I have got this man Montmorency, what shall I do with him?' I knew a lot about the sewers in London – I had done work about Victorian engineering in London long, long ago, and it is just a lovely world to make up a story in.

It is the good old-fashioned storytelling technique of going somewhere else – although while I was writing, I didn't analyse in any way what I was doing. I didn't read a lot of older children's books, because of course, as your children get older, you don't read their books, they read them themselves. So I had no idea what the market was. It was just a story my children liked and that everybody told me I should write down. I had gone off and done little bits of research on it, moved house twice, and lost all the notes. That was brilliant: it was actually the best thing that could have happened because it meant that I was not trying to serve my notes. It was all in my head. So I planned and wrote the story, but of course as you are writing, things change. And I go around all the time picking up little facts and things that I might use.

Writing the first book was just an end in itself, but when I got a publisher for it, they wanted more. So I knew there would be another, but not that there would be a third, and fourth, and that I could go on indefinitely now if I wanted to, I think. It becomes easier in the sense that I now feel that I really know the characters so well – almost laying the table for them! So I know how they would react in certain situations, and what is interesting about them. *I* want to know what happens next: I really, really do. They are like my soap opera. I really want the next episode.

I am quite an impatient reader myself, and in a way, when I am writing, I am telling myself the story, and I think that helps make it exciting to read. I don't think it works if you sit down and think, 'Now I am going to write a really good piece of description with lots of metaphors.' I couldn't do that. And what is interesting is that when you revise, and I revise and revise and revise, I find that the pieces I cut out are usually the bits I have been most proud of when I first wrote them! You really have to teach yourself to do that and to forget that you stayed up all night writing a bit, if, when you read it, you think it is no good, or that it would be very much better if it was like it was when you first did it, before you started playing around with it.

I have got two jobs, as well as lots of other little things that I kept up with when I had children, such as being trustee of the charity Listening Books. Fortunately I am doing research, so I am master of my own time, but because of that, I have got to manage my time very well. So I tend to work in huge blocks supplemented by grabbed time: I suddenly realize I have got a bit of time I wasn't expecting. I think I am quite an efficient worker because I am always so grateful to have the time. I haven't got time to have writer's block. There is quite a big driving force in me and it probably comes partly from when I worked as a journalist, always having deadlines. Now I have to set my own deadlines, but I am pretty good at sticking to them, because I have lived the consequences of not doing that, and it is not pretty.

I am not someone who says, 'I do so many hours a day', because I can't, in that I have to do other things as well. I do an awful lot of work at night. My husband goes to work in the middle of the night. Quite often, I haven't gone to bed by the time he leaves, and he will come in and say, 'Did you realize it is three in the morning?', and I won't have realized. Or, I have been to bed, and he gets up and I can't get back to sleep, so I get up and work. I *love* working at night, because the phone doesn't ring, family aren't around, there are no distractions, and I can literally forget what I am doing. I can sit down, maybe at ten o'clock at night and start working and then think, 'What are those birds?' and it is the dawn chorus coming up, and I haven't moved, which is awful, because then you can't move! Somebody told me you should move every 20 minutes, but I think if I did that I might go back to bed.

You have to be careful, because although you are in this strange, trance-like state, you can do a lot of bad stuff in the night if you are very tired. The best thing is if you are working at night, but not from a basis of total exhaustion. I find it is very easy to focus on the one task then. I write at a computer, although I do a lot of the planning stages with pencil and paper. I tend to get normal school notebooks, although there are these French ones you can get that I love, which are foolscap size, and some of them have grid paper, for doing graphs. I like those because it keeps my writing a bit neater and straight.

I plan out how the story goes in a very visual way: in a very graphic way. I also make charts and timelines of what is going on. Because the plots do get quite intricate, and also if you are referring back to something that happened in a previous book, you need to look and see when someone was born, or when they first met, and was it autumn or winter, if you want to do a flashback. It is quite scribbled, but *I* know what it means. Then when I start writing, although I have the notebook there, I almost never look at it, because I know in my head what it is. Also, while I am writing on the computer, I will keep pencils and paper by me, because I will suddenly have an idea about something ten chapters back, and I will scribble it down.

So I am reasonably organized, although the room where I work is my study but is used for all sorts of other family things as well, so you can imagine what it is like. Also I have got this huge problem at the moment that my computer is terribly overloaded so it keeps crashing and so I have got to get a new one and I can't bear the idea of not having the stuff I know. I work on a laptop in libraries when I go researching. I might be working on my normal work, of which a lot is transcribing manuscripts, and then if I have got to wait for something to be brought up from the stacks, I will go and do a little bit of reading around the nineteenth century.

At the moment I have finished the third Montmorency, which is at the printers. When it had been copy-edited, and I had to read it through, my youngest daughter, who prefers listening to reading, wanted to hear it. So I recorded it onto her i-Pod as I corrected the proofs, and it turned out a brilliant way to correct proofs, because it makes you read slowly enough to spot the mistakes. It is also a terribly good discipline for how you structure your sentences, and where you put your commas and things like that, because you realize when it is not flowing. So I think for the next book, I will do that at a much earlier stage. I am thinking about the fourth book now. I am letting Montmorency get older, which is quite unusual. He will be getting on for 50, and he may get older still. But I think it is quite nice for children to read about someone of that age. They are surrounded by people of 50, so why should they only be fed a diet of children and teenagers and adults who are 40? So having already crossed the barrier of people not wanting the book originally because there were no children in it, now I have made it even worse!

When I first submitted *Montmorency*, it seemed to me at the time that it was taking ages to get a publisher – about three months, I think – but I know from talking to other authors that that was, in fact, pretty quick. What was frustrating was that those who turned it down generally said that they had enjoyed reading it, but that you simply couldn't have a children's book without child characters. One American editor even suggested making Montmorency a child – which would have been pure nonsense. In the end the editor who bought the book – Kirsty Skidmore at Scholastic – saw no problem whatever. It's easy now to be philosophical and say that everything turned out for the best. I got a wonderful editor, and I wouldn't have wanted to work with those who couldn't see past the conventional, but it is frustrating to think of people simply ticking check boxes of received publishing wisdom about what works and doesn't work, rather than trusting their instincts.

When Scholastic said they wanted a series it presented a certain difficulty, in trying to make the books stand alone as well.

You have to work out how to reintroduce characters that most of your readers probably know already. I choose to do it as we go along, rather than having a huge flashback, but I find it quite difficult: pacing it within the story. I like to hang it on something that is happening in the new story, so something happening might remind a character of an event that happened in a previous book, or someone might speak to someone else about what someone used to be like. I hope they stand alone, but it is a desperately difficult thing to judge yourself. That is why having good editors and agents to read is important, although they, too, of course, get to know too much.

I have people who read for me before the book goes anywhere – mainly my kids and Jim, although he doesn't have much time. I found that one of the difficult things is that you are very possessive about your manuscript. You think it is great, but you have got to make yourself able to take criticism and constructive suggestions. And you do make catastrophic mistakes. I mean, I make terrible errors of calling someone by the wrong name – nothing really major like forgetting I have sent them to Scotland or something like that; but little things that someone else will pick up. So you have to open yourself up to saying, 'Please look at this and don't flatter me, please tell me.' But at the same time, the message you are giving out is, 'Please flatter me. I have been slaving on this and I want you to tell me it is the greatest book you have ever read.' So you have to line up your people that you can trust. Children are brilliant because they don't care a damn about flattering you.

I have been quite lucky with reviews: I haven't had a stinking bad one. Actually, I haven't had that many, because children's books don't get reviewed that much. When *Montmorency* was in proof form, the publishers sent the proofs off to various people to read and Stephen Fry was one of them. He sent a *fantastic* review of it back: I almost sleep with it under my pillow it was so nice! So then I contacted him informally and asked if he would like to do the tape of the book. The tape was being sold to the BBC at the time, and they contacted him as well, and he agreed, which was wonderful, because he really *got* the book. I desperately wanted it to be read by somebody who *liked* it, and I knew he was a fantastic reader because he had read Harry Potter. I feel like he is in my house every night because there is always a Harry Potter tape on, or a Montmorency tape going, so his voice just booms around the stairwell.

My youngest child, who is 13, listens more than she reads. I think she is addicted to the Harry Potter tapes. She is almost not listening, because her tape machine automatically turns the tape over, so you have to sometimes just go into her room and turn it off. She must nearly know them off by heart, except the ones that have got broken, so she has those with bits missing. It was very funny when I first heard Stephen Fry reading my stuff; it almost sounded to me like Harry Potter because it was the same voice. But I love the way he reads the books: it is really a perfect marriage, I think, for me. There isn't a single place where he is reading against the text. You also get a lot of children's book reading which is patronizing with silly voices. Stephen does gorgeous voices for all my people – good real voices. And he is absolutely meticulous about getting the same voice across the books. The second tape hasn't come out yet, but I have heard it and it is just lovely.

Apart from the Montmorency books, I have written two short stories recently. They were both commissioned, so in a sense the different genre was thrust upon me. One is in a collection called *Thirteen* which is 13 writers writing stories about being 13, set in the modern age. That was huge fun, and was done in the first person, which I don't do at all in *Montmorency*, where I am a kind of helicopter above the whole thing. The other one is a war story to mark the sixtieth anniversary of the end of the Second World War. That is historical, and is about a family who all survive the First World War but is completely wrecked by what happened.

It is about the effects of war on the survivors, because I thought everyone else in the anthology would be writing about the dead people. It didn't have the same swashbuckling feel that *Montmorency* might have: it is quite dark.

I have another 18 months to do on this PhD and I am *desperate* for it to be finished, but I don't feel I can just walk away from it. But when it is finished, I think I will regard myself as a full-time writer. Then I will do more, because I have ideas all the time for other things, and I love the idea of writing them. I was always good at writing, and ironically, I wonder if one of the reasons why is because I didn't read a lot: I was read to a lot. My mother was very good at reading out loud. So certainly, when I write, I hear it. I write at listening pace. I think some people write, and almost see it as print as they write, but I hear it and see it in action, but don't see the words as a shape.

I went to a school that was very hot on creative writing, and I've got a video at home, taken from an old black-and-white film done by ITN, of me reading a story I wrote in 1959. It is in an item about homework, and my wonderful headmistress of my primary school is saying how she will have no truck with homework or the 11-plus! I am desperate that kids do so much narrow work now that they don't get a chance to write. We wrote a lot at school and I used to make up stories then. I was always very, very shy of it though, and even at school, I remember getting my best friend to submit a poem to the school magazine in her name, that I had written, because I was embarrassed about doing it. And I have left it very late in life to start doing it publicly, too. I would never, ever, have submitted a manuscript to anyone when I was younger. I thought writers were other people.

I think what is nice now is that people at school do get a lot of writers coming round, and they do see that writers are just normal people. So there may be a lot more writing going on in the future. Although they do see that we don't make any money as well. I am always asked, 'How much money do you make?'

because of J. K. Rowling, and they are flabbergasted when they hear how little it is. So I don't think anyone would take it as a career choice. But in a way, I have always done this sort of thing. At the BBC I made films and programmes, which is the same kind of craft: keeping someone interested. Yet I have felt a bit like I am inventing the wheel, because I am not from a writerly circle, and haven't written before. You do get lots of invitations to go to sessions about 'How we write' and I am a bit spooked by those. I have a feeling that if I prod this balloon too hard it might just burst and it is better not to analyse too hard what makes it work.

I am proud of the Montmorency books in the way I am proud of my kids. I *love* Montmorency, and Fox-Selwyn and Vi. I have really, really got to like George Fox-Selwyn terribly much. I am in agonies with the doctor: he is so well-meaning, but he does things that are quite wrong sometimes. Then some of the minor characters are quite fun. There is one character in book three, who has a lot of rather unpleasant features, and most of those features have been lifted from a person I know, and exaggerated of course. I know the person concerned hasn't noticed, and that can be quite nice – getting your revenge on some irritating habit!

Another thing I am glad of is that I think the books manage to be historically based without being overtly historically instruc-tive. I don't want them to be like textbooks. The reason I base them in the past is that it is so much easier. If you are trying to write an exciting story, it is much easier to set it in a time when there were no telephones, no email. In the second book for example, while they are going up and down to Scotland, they don't know what is going on in London until the news reaches them. Having this island has turned out to be hugely great, because they can be totally isolated there. I think the reason there has been this huge plunge into fantasy as a genre is that you can set up a world where it is exciting. These days, you are almost never in a position of not knowing. It can be wonderful in some ways, to be, say, stuck on a tube train, and not know what is going on, and have to find out when you get out.

The reason I write is *almost* the reason some people turn to drugs or drink. It is my private, out-of-this-world thing. I am completely in control of it, but particularly in the night-time sessions of writing, I am completely away. I can make it knock out all the things I am worried about in the real world. In the story I know where everyone is standing in the room: I could do a film script tomorrow of it. A lot of people who write say they have problems, not with the big plot, but managing the scenes – who is in, or out of the room. I have no trouble with that whatever. I literally can see them there. I know where they are, and where the window and door is, what the furniture and pictures are like. I don't describe all this in the books, but I know it, and while I am writing, it blots out everything else. That is the addiction for me. It is also habitual. I am not a smoker, but I think about Montmorency all the time, almost like having a cigarette. It is always, 'What would he be doing now? Could he do this? Could he do that?' I am sure that when I go dotty, when I am old, I will be talking to him. I will be introducing him to people! It is *terrifyingly* real.

# Naomi Wallace

*A poet turned playwright, Naomi Wallace was born in Kentucky, and now lives in Yorkshire. Her plays have premiered in theatres such as the Traverse and the Bush in the United Kingdom and the Humana Festival at Louisville, USA. She has also written for the Royal Shakespeare Company in London and had work performed at the Joseph Papp Public Theatre in New York. Her film* Lawn Dogs, *produced by Duncan Kenworthy* (Four Weddings and a Funeral), *opened at the London Film Festival, having won the Best Screenplay award at the Sitges Film Festival. Her work has won much acclaim. Her awards for theatre include the Susan Smith Blackburn Prize, the Kesselring Prize and an OBIE Award. In 1999 (still in her 30s) she was the recipient of the prestigious MacArthur Fellowship, the grant popularly known as the genius award.*

*Naomi Wallace's plays cover an enormous range. Just a few examples are works set in the American Depression; the Iraq War; the Great Plague in London; 1760s Yorkshire, when Capability and Asquith Brown attempted to change the landscape of England. What her plays have in common is sparseness of language, tension, violence, eroticism, a colliding of the past and present, and a combination of reality and dream. Her work also exhibits her concerns with issues of class, gender, race, exploitation and dysfunction. On the whole, however, optimism prevails in that there is resistance to injustice, the future is challenged, and love is seen to be stronger than war.*

## Selected Bibliography

Plays
*The War Boys* (1993), *In the Heart of America* (1994), *One Flea Spare* (1995), *Slaughter City* (1996), *The Trestle at Pope Lick Creek* (1998), *The Inland Sea* (2002)

Film
*Lawn Dogs* (1997)

Poetry
*To Dance a Stony Field* (1995)

This exchange is from *In The Heart of America* (Act One, scene 11). The play is set in the Gulf War of 1990 and in Vietnam in 1969. In this extract, two soldiers are fighting in the Kuwaiti desert and fall in love. Both characters are male and in their early 20s – Craver is Anglo-American; Remzi, Palestinian-American:

CRAVER: I had a thing for the Sentry jet, but how long can love last, after the first kiss, after the second, still around after the third? I dumped the Sentry jet and went on to the Wild Weasel, F-4G. Like a loyal old firehorse, the Weasel was back in action.
REMZI: Have you ever touched the underbelly of a recon plane? Two General Electric J79-15 turbojets.
CRAVER: If you run your hand along its flank, just over the hip, to the rear end, it will go wet. Not damp but I mean wet.
REMZI: Have you ever run your face over the wing of an A-6 Intruder, or opened your mouth onto the tail of a AV-8B Harrier II? It's not steel you taste. It's not metal.
CRAVER: Ever had a Phoenix missile at the tip of your tongue? Nine hundred and eighty-five pounds of power, at launch.

*        *        *

I started writing poetry when I was very little; at about six or seven I would bring poems to my teachers in the hopes that they would like me. I wrote poetry pretty seriously up until I was in my early 30s, which is when I wrote my first play. I remember reading a play by a good friend of mine, Lisa Schlesinger, and thinking, 'Oh! I can do something like this!' But I think it was already in me, because I found the writing of poetry very isolating and solitary, and a lot of my poems at that point were what some people call persona poems, or dramatic voices. So I realized I could do that on the stage.

Up until that time I was not a theatre-goer, and didn't really read plays, so I was kind of an outsider to theatre. I think I was in my early 20s when I went to a real theatre that was outside of high school, and I found it extremely intimidating. It was actually the Actors Theatre of Louisville, in the late 70s. It has changed a lot since then, but at that time, everyone was so dressed up, and it seemed so formal and stuffy, and I just didn't like it. It took me about ten years after that to change my mind about theatre.

I took the programme at University of Iowa, and realized that there could be a different kind of theatre – I think I had only seen mainstream theatre. When I realized I could write what interested *me* for the theatre, it changed my vision completely. I also began to find other writers who were interested to write for the theatre the way I was. Both my poetry and my plays have always been fairly simple and robust. I prefer the word 'lyric' to 'poetic' as a description of my plays, because poetic seems to imply walking on tiptoes.

I know that inspiration is a valuable, perhaps necessary part of writing, but I am very unromantic in those terms. I feel there is so much written about writers waking to scribble in their closet in the wee hours, and the characters are calling to them from the yard. That stuff doesn't really interest me. When writing a play, I usually start with an idea of the subject. This idea usually comes out of either being moved, or angered, by something in history, or a relationship within communities, or something where I think, 'I want to know more about this. How did this come to be?'

For example, I recently wrote a short play called *A State of Innocence,* which is about an Israeli soldier who is shot by a sniper in Gaza and dies in the doorway of a Palestinian home, and the Palestinian mother holds him while he dies. Now that is something I read, and was just stunned by it, and thought, 'How did a situation like this arise, where two people were somehow able to connect against all odds? And how can I write about that without being sentimental or sloppy, and keep alive the fact that the next day their house was bulldozed anyway?' That was one incident which inspired me, but it is often through reading history, or accounts of conflict, that I find a moment where they are very personalized.

For something like *A State of Innocence,* once I decided to write it, I had a lot of the play worked out in advance, although not actually written down. I knew it was going to be about a soldier in the zoo in Gaza, and he thinks he is still alive. A Palestinian woman is visiting him and he thinks he is just guarding the zoo, and then gradually, through their conversation, he would realize he was dead, and that she was visiting him in her mind. I knew that would happen, and I knew that in the end he would try to deny that he was dead, and I knew the last image would be the actual one of her holding him.

On the other hand, when I wrote *In the Heart of America,* all I knew was that it would begin with a man standing on his head, and something about the end, and maybe a couple of central images. I didn't know how it was going to play out. Now I keep note cards of acts and scenes, and although I still don't stick closely to that, I do more than I used to – perhaps some of my plays have become more complicated.

It interests me to write plays that take place in the past, not only because I feel that the past informs the present, but because I think it gives us a little distance. Things aren't over-determined as they can become in a dialogue about contemporary conflict. Often my writing comes out of a challenge to myself.

For instance, how does one talk about class relations, without using that language on stage? Out of that came *One Flea Spare* [set in 1665: 'another example of fine, ambitious writing . . . The London Plague is evoked in statistics and the overwhelming reality of quirky, Marivaux-like social role reversals in a single room.' Michael Coveney, the *Observer*] and specifically the scene where Mr Snelgrave [a wealthy elderly man] gets Bunce [a young sailor] to try on his shoes.

There is some talk of history in there, but that came out of reading Caryl Churchill's *Top Girls*, where she launches into a discussion about Thatcher's Britain at the end of the play, and thinking that worked wonderfully. Caryl Churchill did it with the language, and was able to build up to it, so it felt like an integral part of the play. So I thought, 'How can I do it in a different way, so that those relations are brought to the forefront, without talking about class relations directly?' And I did it with the shoes. Issues of power have always interested me, because there cannot be conflict without them. I have always been interested in negotiations over power, exploitation, fighting, exchanges of power.

My children have said, 'How do you write about war, when you have never been in a war?' I think all writers (and actors, too) access their own history, loss and trauma, that all of us have in our lives, in order to connect with the situation or history that is outside their own, so that they can relate to it emotionally. But I do do a lot of research. Many years ago I was talking to a playwright (I don't want to say the name), and she proudly asserted, 'I never do research'. And I remember, when I was still beginning, wondering, 'Does that put me in a lesser category?' But it has come to be the way I have continued to educate myself, growing up in a system that basically de-educates us, in terms of our own histories and the histories of the world, certainly about class and race issues. Usually I am interested in something because I know very little about it, so that what I get, besides writing a play, is an education in that period, and about those issues.

I even add a bibliography or 'further readings' at the end of my plays. I do it because historians and cultural critics have been some of the people who have inspired me the most, and I feel I need to acknowledge their work. For instance, my play *Things of Dry Hours*, which will be produced in spring 2006 in New York, was inspired by a book by Robin Kelley called *Hammer and Hoe*, about Alabama in the 1930s. Robin Kelley is a black cultural critic; probably, I think, the best cultural critic and historian in the United States at the moment. His book was about blacks running the Communist Party in Alabama, working with a few whites. That countered the whole surface history we have of communism in the United States being amongst intellectuals in New York, who were all a bunch of puppets for the Soviet Union.

Again, for me, it was the same feeling of 'What were these mostly illiterate, very poor, black people doing, risking their lives to be part of the Communist Party?' Well, they had a very different vision of the United States, and I thought, 'Wow! How did they get to that point, that they could have such a radically different vision?' So then I began reading about the period, but a lot of the work draws off that book. There is also a woman called Tera Hunter, who wrote about black women in a book called *To Joy My Freedom*, which was another inspiration for the play.

As I have gone on with my work, I have become more aware of how crucial contemporary historians are to my writing, and I want to acknowledge that. But also, I have always felt that if you are a 'left-wing writer', if one wants to label me that, you need to do twice as much research. You need to get it right, and I am also convinced that you need to write twice as well, if you are to be believed. I don't add a bibliography necessarily to shore up my work, but I do it to allow people to look at the sources and if they are interested, go beyond the theatrical experience. Start reading! Get interested!

I write because I have always felt grateful that I have a career in which I am able to do something that I want to do. I may not always enjoy it: I might find it frightening at times, and extremely frustrating. Usually before any new play I will have just decided that it is impossible for me to ever write again! But as writers, we throw a lot of tantrums. I think people who write for the theatre are the most egotistical of all artists. We want our work not just to be read, or thought about, we want it heard, loud, by a large communal audience. And we want our language inside the bodies of other people, and have them uttering it out loud: now if that isn't invasive, I don't know what is!

Much has been said about why there are so few women play-wrights and screenplay writers, and now it is a kind of 'dirty conversation' – thought of as unfashionable and tedious. The arts are supposed to be where women have excelled, but more and more, it very much parallels hiring practices outside the theatre world. Men get most jobs, and white women get more jobs than women of colour. Every time I see the statistics of new plays produced, the number of women writers is at less than 25 per cent. Then the higher up the ladder you go, to West End or Broadway, the more white and male it becomes.

I mainly write plays rather than screenplays, and they have been performed usually in smaller theatres. But money constraints, like having a limited number of cast, or one set, do not really affect my writing. I did have a recent commission for the National Theatre, where I was able to say, 'OK I can go bigger', and that applied too when I wrote *The Inland Sea*, which was originally written for the Royal Shakespeare Company and went to the Oxford Stage Company. But generally, I seem to have written a small play followed by a bigger play, and then a small one again. I tend to write in a way that can be produced in a small or large theatre, and trust that a good director will find a way to do it anywhere.

I am not interested in realism on stage: it is a lie anyway, it is just an imitation of reality. In my texts virtually all the settings are described as 'non-realistic'. I have always been interested in showing the constructedness of theatre, and I like very bare stages. One of the reasons is that the language I use could be called heightened, and it brings its own furniture with it. On a clear stage, the body of the actor, and the language, have a lot of space.

I do not write many stage directions in the script, but I do sometimes write '*beat*' to indicate a pause, or I might add a stop in what would normally be mid-sentence. All language is rhetorical in some sense, and if the character has to say something like 'I love you', or 'I despise you', which you can't make original, one way of hearing it in a fresh way is through the rhythm. So you could say, 'I. Love you.' Or 'I love. You', which brings a different sensibility to an old phrase. We are stuck with the language that is diminished and perverted on a daily basis through materialism and commercialism, so unpredictable pauses might sometimes help.

My plays also tend not to have a linear structure. My first play was straight realism, and then I went for more radical form, because I felt that I was not able to present what I wanted in following the traditional Aristotelian structure, although of course it is still in my plays. Sometimes it is challenged Aristotelian structure, or inverted. Letting the past have as much present as the lived moment, means using a structure that allows a shuffle between past, present and future, that doesn't follow a more traditional or realistic form.

One of the things I love about theatre, and it ties in with my interest in the past, is that the theatre is the only place where, for me, the past, the present, or the future, can be in the same moment. Whether it is through ghosts, people meeting each other from the past and the future, or whatever it may be. Real time, the present, on stage, is very malleable. I often have ghosts and time-travellers in my plays, interacting with people in the present. I feel it is a way of bringing the past forcefully into the present in a very alive way. And I probably find the dead more 'alive' than the living. And to embody the past on stage, one needs to do it through the body.

I have challenged myself recently to say, 'OK, no ghosts!' In the play I wrote for the National – I just finished the first draft – there are no ghosts, except one does make an appearance, but only in one scene. Because as a writer there are things that we know how to do easily, and each time I write a play, I try to challenge myself not to use my 'top ten greatest hits' under simply a different guise. Some people are born to do a lot of things well. I think that what I can do better than I can do some other things is write, and so I try to do that as well as I can.

I feel very privileged in that I also write for film, and I have steady commissions coming in. There are a lot of writers who have to hold two jobs in the beginning, in order to be able to write, because they are not getting paid for their writing. I have always felt really lucky. But I have read so much hogwash about how you have to write every day and set certain hours, and I think most writers who really do it for a living have their own methods, and there is no set rule. I have three children, and you have to work around that. You don't just go off in a moment of inspiration and leave everybody without dinner. And women everywhere who work have that same issue.

I don't write every day. I am usually doing some kind of research, or reading, towards a project. I usually spend a couple of years doing research – not eight hours a day, but collecting materials, reading and taking notes. Then I am not someone who writes the first draft of a play over a long period: that is something I have found intolerable. What I'll do is give myself four weeks. I feel I am a 'pressure cooker writer'. When I am ready to write something, I will write an outline, and then pick a day, and know that in one month I will have my play. Then in a mad attack of blind faith I begin writing. The first draft is always the major labour. Rewriting, I enjoy, because you have already got it; you are just improving, and rearranging, and writing new scenes.

Some of my plays will have seven pretty serious drafts. The changes may have been big, or small, but they are serious changes enough that I kept the draft. But there might also be a lot of changing in between that. I think a lot of the good work happens in rewriting. When my children were younger I did it on computer, and I liked being able to get that first draft already on the computer. But the last play I wrote by hand. I just decided to go back to notebooks. I had some resistance at first, and now I am so glad I did. I think it is something Edward Said talked about in his last years, how we have lost this intimacy with the materiality of actually writing, with the pen, or pencil, and paper. I like the mobility and I also like seeing it written again and seeing the actual changes with the words crossed out. So I think I am going to stick with that. The last few small pieces, I have also written a rough draft on paper.

Usually I only write a play every couple of years, but in the last six months I have written two, because of commission deadlines. My most recent play, called *On The Wall*, is for the Guthrie Theatre of Minneapolis, and I am writing with two other writers: a Palestinian writer and a Jewish American writer. We wrote outlines, because there were three of us, and I didn't find it restrictive, I found it very helpful.

I have also written film scripts collaboratively, with my husband, Bruce McLeod. We usually have a synopsis or outline, and note cards, and then we pick which scenes we each want to write. We do something I call over-writing. For instance, I will write the first scenes of a film, and Bruce will write the next three, but he will read my three over, before he does his. And we have an agreement that you are allowed to change anything in the other person's scenes that you feel strongly about, unless the person who wrote it feels so strongly, like, 'Where's my brilliant line? I'm putting it back in!', which rarely happens. You have to not work with your ego. Then you get a kind of blended text, but of course it has to be a writer of your own sensibilities. My husband has often written lines of my plays, too, if I am stuck, or if I am introducing a new character and need a slightly different voice.

I also remember when Tony Kushner [who wrote *Angels in America*] was directing *In the Heart of America*, and there were a couple of lines that just weren't working, and I said, 'Tony, I am so burnt out with rewriting, why don't you just write that couple of lines?' He didn't hesitate a moment, and I love that, because I know where his couple of lines are, and I have never felt possessive of my work in that way. It doesn't happen that often, but if an actor suggests a change in a line, and I like it better, I'll do it. When I wrote poetry I lived this kind of myth that I enjoyed working alone, and to my surprise I found that was completely false – I love working with other people, and being part of a larger project with actors, a director and designer.

For the world premiere of a piece I get very involved. If it is a bigger show, I will tend to work with the director on rewrites before rehearsals begin. But after a show's first couple of productions, I just let it go for people to do the way they want to. The only way I am involved is to say 'yes' or 'no' to the company who wants to produce it, and I almost always say 'yes'. Which brings me to the question of whether writers should let anybody do their work who wants to. I don't on the first round, but I remember another playwright sharing with me, 'I never let universities do my work, because they do such bad productions.' I feel the opposite.

It doesn't matter to me any more if they do a bad show: it is the people involved – how they can have a changing experience, what they can learn. It is not just looking at the show as the final product. My work, although it has received numerous awards in the United States, has not received the kind of regional productions that a lot of plays have by playwrights of the same standing. But one of the best-sellers published by Broadway Plays is *One Flea Spare*, because they are teaching it at the university. So it is being bought for classes, and I am as happy about that as about a show. If people are reading the work, and thinking about it, especially young people, I am thrilled. It doesn't matter to me ultimately if there was a show in Louisiana that got bad reviews and it was a terrible director.

There was a time when the United States was behind Britain in giving my plays space to be on the stage. I was sort of discovered in the British theatre before the US theatre. My local theatre is the Actors Theatre of Louisville, which is a big regional theatre in the United States, and they had known about my work for years, but it was only after the Royal Shakespeare Company did *Slaughter City*, that they decided to do one of my plays. Then ironically, they decided to do my British play, *One Flea Spare*.

It is not really for me to say whether theatres view my plays as subversive, or what, but now, it is pretty equal in terms of productions in both countries, which I am glad about. I do feel still that British theatre is more open to my work. This spring, *A State of Innocence* was done, about the Israeli soldier, and we hadn't been able to get an important fringe theatre in New York, or an off-Broadway theatre to do it. But it is now going to be done in San Francisco by a Middle-Eastern theatre company.

On the other hand, the play I have been working on most recently, now called *Rawal Pindi*, for the National Theatre in London, has just been turned down. The play is about Pakistan, and I turned it in right after the bombings in London [in July 2005], and it is clear from their letter that they passed on it for political reasons. I have kept that letter: it is very important to me. I had pitched the idea, and they had commissioned me, and Nick Hytner [director] said he loved the idea, and my work. But they haven't taken it any further than the first draft. So it will now go out to other theatres, and hopefully another theatre will be interested in it.

It was upsetting to me because I have always admired Nicholas Hytner, and the National, and the least they could have done was take it to the developmental stage. They just basically said that my view of Britain's relationship with Pakistan wasn't resonant to them. They loved my main characters, but said the lesser characters didn't ring true. But I felt, 'Well, big deal. It's a first draft!' That wasn't the reason it was turned down. The two main characters are Pakistani, and that is one of the reasons Nicholas Hytner wanted it. He said it would be wonderful, and we could bring in a whole different audience to the National Theatre, and we could get a big soap-opera star – but, well, that was it. My kids always say, 'Mummy, why can't you just write something commercial?' And sometimes I think, 'Why the hell didn't I, you know?'

I am not just a writer: I am also white, and I grew up in relative privilege to most people. But I have decided that I am not going to write for a white, privileged theatre, and what that means is that I am not just going to write for white actors. The challenge, and the possibility of going wrong with that, is big, because I am writing against my own white mind. I am attempting to write inclusive theatre, recognizing that I was brought up in a racist, homophobic society in the United States. I am excited by it, because I am continually challenged with my own distorted lens. I know there can be real difficulties with people writing outside their own experience and especially their race.

One of the great abuses in both American and British theatre is white writers' history of writing for people who are not white. I like learning from that, and learning to be humble, and realizing my own blind spots. One thing happened for me recently, which made me feel it was all worth it. I wrote a short play called *The Retreating World* that has been done quite often in Europe and the United States, which is told from the voice of an ex-Iraqi soldier after the first Gulf war. It was done at the American University of Cairo, in English. The main theatre critic from Cairo came and wrote about her experience of seeing this play. She wrote that first she was sure that it was written by an Iraqi writer in exile, then it was an Arab-American, and she wrote about her shock that it was a white woman from Kentucky who had written this, and her gladness that the play was there, and how much she liked it.

For me that was such a gift, because with all the mistakes I probably did make, I was able to connect with another culture and another people in a way that seemed authentic. That made me glad. Recently too, when *Things of Dry Hours* was done, an actor I very much admire, Lisa Gay Hamilton, read it, and wrote a letter to someone else, which was passed on to me, in which she thought I was a black woman. Even though, actually, there was some disappointment, I felt good, because theatre still doesn't do black women's work the way it should, nor allow them the space and support to do it. So here comes this white woman, who has more space and support, and writes about this history.

So there are a lot of contradictions involved, but I feel glad when I can come out of the box that I was taught in, and supposed to stay in, I assume. But I am not congratulating myself in any way. My God, I have learned so much from other theatre artists, especially ones that are not white, about where I have used stereotypes, where I have to learn, where I am blind – and I love that! It doesn't bother my ego: either I don't have one, or it is so huge it doesn't bother me. I just figure all the learning I can get will make me a better writer. When I write about people and cultures outside of my race and class (my mother's family was working class, my father's was privileged), and when I get it right, or it is able to speak to the folks about whom I am writing – that to me, makes it feel worthwhile.

The piece I chose to quote is from *In the Heart of America* and Craver is Anglo-American and Remzi is Palestinian-American.

It is a moment in my work where these two men are talking about love and desire, but the only language at their disposal is military language, the language of death. The contradiction in that shows something that I am trying to do in my work. Also it is a sexy bit, and I like that. I have always placed the body as central in my work: the labouring body, the destroyed body, the resisting body. We live in our bodies and all experience is through our bodies, so everything is connected. In *In the Heart of America*, they are going out destroying other bodies, and at the same time, trying to touch each other's in an act of love.

The body is an erotic machine, sometimes depleted, deformed, or oppressed, but continually fighting back against that. I have always been interested in the transforming capacities of eroticism and desire. We can sometimes put the emphasis on 'we can all fuck our way to liberation', which sadly isn't true. As much as our minds have been censored, so have our bodies. We are taught in a very rigid manner, how to love, who to love, where to touch, how we can make love, and desire often crosses these boundaries, or breaks the rules. Heterosexuals are probably the most rigid, so thank God for other sexualities that have helped liberate heterosexuals!

# Benjamin Zephaniah

*Benjamin Zephaniah, born in Birmingham in 1958, grew up in Jamaica and Handsworth, and was sent to an approved school for uncontrollable, rebellious children in Shropshire. He finished full-time education at 13, dyslexic and unable to read or write, and ended up in jail for burglary. But after prison, he turned from crime to music and poetry. He moved to London in 1979 and published his first poetry collection in 1980. Zephaniah writes out of a sense of urgency and a commitment to social justice, poems strongly influenced by the music and poetry of Jamaica, which are intended to be recited or performed, rather than read. As in the poetry of ancient cultures, rhythmic flow and phonic patterns create a close relationship between sound and meaning.*

*Zephaniah has inspired many of the new generation of rappers, and of all the performance poets that emerged in the late 70s and early 80s he is one of the few that is still going strong. But he is not just an immensely popular poet. In 1998 the University of North London awarded him an honorary doctorate in recognition of his work; he was made a Doctor of Letters by the University of Central England in 1999; made Doctor of the University of Staffordshire in 2002; Ealing Hospital in London named a ward after him; he turned down an OBE.*

*Zephaniah believes that working with human rights groups, animal rights groups and other political organizations means that he will never lack subject matter. He has worked for the British Council, come under fire in Gaza and met Mandela. But while his poems cover domestic and international concerns, they include humour, word-play and parody. Zephaniah has also produced numerous music recordings, and written stage and radio plays. He is a familiar figure on television, having appeared on programmes ranging from* The Bill *and* EastEnders *to* Blue Peter *and* Question Time. *Youthful-looking, with long dreadlocks, he speaks with a Birmingham drawl punctuated by laughter, and effortlessly recites extracts from his poems while in conversation.*

## Selected Bibliography

Poetry
*Pen Rhythm* (1980), *Talking Turkeys* (1994), *Propa Propaganda* (1996), *Too Black, Too Strong* (2001), *We are Britain!* (2002)

Novels for Teenagers
*Face* (1999), *Refugee Boy* (2001)

Records
*Us and Dem* (1990), *Belly of the Beast* (1996)

Plays
*Playing the Right Tune* (1985), *Dread Poets Society* (1991)

The following are the third and fourth stanzas of 'Naked' – an 18-stanza poem in *Too Black, Too Strong*. This book includes poems written while Zephaniah was working as Poet in Residence at the chambers of London barrister Michael Mansfield, at the time of the Stephen Lawrence case and other high-profile political trials:

Dis is me, hungry for the priceless forbidden, looking
    for the man who wrote the superhighway code
    so that I can rob his richness.
    He got insurance, he got the state, let me get him.
    I wanna find game show hosts and put
    the bastards on trial. I wanna kill educated ignorance.

Dis is me naked, revolting in front of you, I'm
   not much but I give a damn. Lovers look
   at me, haters look at me as I exhibit
   my love and my fury on dis desperate
   stage.

\*      \*      \*

In the poem called 'Naked' I try to strip myself bare and be as honest and personal as I can. I am such a political person that I find it very hard to be personal without being political, because I think it is all linked. If I get affected by seeing poverty, it *is* personal. People ask, 'Why don't you write more love poems?' but I think my poems are love poems, because they are about loving humanity.

The first line here is about me always wondering why things are legal or illegal, and banned and forbidden. I am of the belief that if Adam and Eve were in the Garden of Eden, and they had this fruit of life, and Eve ate of it, it wasn't an apple; it was sex. Why was it forbidden? Because it made life, and that was a secret that God wanted to keep to himself. So I am interested in things that are forbidden. When I say 'looking / for the man who wrote the superhighway code / so that I can rob of his richness', if you think about Islam, for instance, where the woman is veiled because a man might look at her and lust after her, it is the man who wrote the rule who has got the problem. It is the man who is lusting, and who should go and get therapy! It is as though you were walking along the road and saw a man who might rob you, but you were the one that got punished.

When I talk about putting game show hosts on trial and killing educated ignorance, it is about the façade of things we see, that we think is normal, and people who make rules, and prizes you win and rewards you get for being good. So when I say 'Dis is me naked' it is me trying to be as honest as I can. I am really exhibiting my love and my anger. It is saying that when I am on stage, I am trying to give you all of me.

There is a critic who hates me – I am not sure why. I have been told various things, like it is partly jealousy, or he doesn't like a black poet being so popular. He is black, by the way, so it is not a racial thing. Anyway, I read something by him the other day, where he criticizes me, and thinks I don't write personally, and am too much on my political soapbox. But he ended the article by saying there was one moment of real insight, I think he even used the word genius, which is the poem 'Naked'. I thought it was really interesting that he didn't criticize that poem because he thought that was me being honest.

I have 'done' poetry since I was a child: heard and said it – not read or written it. It was the oral tradition. All my early poetry was hearing it. I heard my mother doing poetry, not my father, so much. It was mainly the women: aunties, and my mother and her friends used to recite poems. Also, they would get tapes of poetry from Jamaica, and again it was mainly women, doing this performance poetry. So that was the first poetry that I heard. Before I even knew it was called poetry, I just loved what people could do with words and sounds. Even as a kid, I noticed that you could say a sentence twice, and depending on the stress you put on it, the meaning could be different. That was why, later on in life, I had to deal with the differences of writing for the page and writing for the stage.

There was also the church. A lot of black soul singers started in the church. This is our equivalent to a white, academic poet, who had a good education, and whose parents read to him. A lot of black singers will say they learnt singing in church. It was the same thing for me, in a way. I learnt the art of performing from watching the preachers. They would sometimes say, 'Get up and say something, boy.' And I knew how to get up and say, 'People watch out, because Jesus is coming. He is coming today!' Or whatever it was. I would just get up and improvise around the theme.

There is a West-African word, 'griot'. Usually, you get a family of griots, but they don't have to be families. The griot is a person who travels from village to village, performing poems, singing songs, maybe acting out a little scene. She or he is also a kind of political agitator. They would also tell the news, especially if there is a famine in another village, or it looks like malaria is spreading, or whatever. In English there isn't a word that covers it. 'Bard', 'troubadour' and 'travelling musician' are not quite right. Sometimes, if I perform poetry, and then go on a programme like *Question Time*, people ask, 'What are you? Do you want to be a poet or a musician, or a politician?' And I say, 'No, I don't want to be a politician. I go on the programme because I care.'

I am always having to justify myself. But when I perform in Africa, I never get those questions asked. The questions I will get asked are, 'What is it like trying to do this tradition in the West? Do they understand you?' It doesn't happen so much now, because people are beginning to understand me, but they used to say, if I wrote a play, or a novel, 'You shouldn't do that: you are a poet.' I write because I want to tell *my* story, because I cannot afford to leave it to a priest, or politician, or spokesperson, to speak on my behalf. I am not a person who writes poetry: I am a poet. I am not an oral poet, or a literary poet. If I wanted to be pedantic about it, I would say that oral poetry is much older than writing poetry down. Why do people judge you by the standard of writing poetry down?

From the cultural place that I come from, if you meet someone in the street, and you tell them you are a poet, they don't turn round and say, 'Oh great! Wonderful! What have you had published?' They say, 'Do it! Show me!' My physical being is the poet, and all the other things are just things I do. Now I am saying a poem, now I'm writing one down, now I'm sharing one, now I'm writing one and am putting it into a play, or a soft-drinks commercial. I write because it is a part of expressing me. And if nobody wanted to hear me, and if no one was interested in buying a Benjamin Zephaniah book, I'd still be a poet. I'd still do it.

Sometimes, if I didn't write a poem, I would be in prison. I feel so much anger, but two things have saved me: poetry and martial arts, which teaches you control. A lot of my poetry is sparked by social injustice, but for different poems, different things come first. Sometimes I have a rhythm, and I feel I am going to find some words to fit that rhythm. At other times I have a subject, but I just haven't found the language to approach it. Sometimes I have something to express, but rap or reggae is going to box me in too much, and so it needs to be freer.

At the moment, I am spending too little time writing poetry. Novels have taken over to a certain extent. Once I start writing a novel, I get so absorbed in it that I find it very difficult to write poetry. I have written a couple of commissioned poems, but I haven't really sat down and been inspired to write a big piece of poetry for about a year or more, which is sad. Sometimes I have just taken some time off, and sat in my study with a blank page in front of me, and said, right, 'What am I feeling? What is touching me? What have I been thinking about lately?' Then there are other times when, for no reason at all, a set of words has come into my head, in a kind of rhythmic form, and that is when I, what I call, 'give birth to a poem': when that happens, it is like a desperate need to release something.

I am a very physical person in that I do a lot of jogging, and kung fu and boxing. Sometimes, because these things involve rhythm, poems can come to me while I do them. For instance, I remember a poem I wrote about money that came to me while I was jogging, and as I think of it now, my feet are going, the rhythm is still there: it came out of listening to my breath and the rhythm of my feet on the ground. 'Money mek a Rich man

feel like a Big man / It mek a Poor man feel like a hooligan . . .'
There are a few poems which I composed completely in my
mind. I do a verse, and then memorize it in my head.

I remember once I was driving from south Wales to London,
and as I was driving I had this inspiration for a poem. I did think,
'Shall I write it down?' but then I had no pen or anything. So as
I was driving, I composed the first verse, and recited it to myself
aloud. It was almost as though I put it in a drawer to one side in
my head, and then did the second verse. Then I put the first verse
and second verse together, and put them back into another
drawer; and did the third verse. When I arrived, I immediately
told it to the person I was meeting, and they said, 'That's good!
Have you got a copy?' and I said, 'I haven't written it down. I just
wrote it in my head.'

So I find different ways of writing, but oral poetry – *hearing* the
sound of it, *feeling* it, the *rhythm* of it, and just composing it in my
head – is I think what I do best. And when it happens, it really is
inspiration taking over. I am sorry to sound a little bit 'arty-farty',
but it is something almost spiritual. I look back on it and I go
'Wow!' With those poems, the first draft tends to be the right one.
When I sit in my study and think and struggle, then I do lots of
rewrites. I do all of it by hand with a pen. I am trying to learn
how to touch-type, and that is OK for novels, but I think when it
is poetry, the paper and a pen is ideal really.

I go through different emotions writing poems. With the poem
I wrote about Stephen Lawrence, for example, I was angry. But a
few years before, that anger would have expressed itself in a dub
poem. Doreen Lawrence, Stephen's mother, knew I was writing
this poem, because we were going to do it on a television programme. So I thought about her, and the way that she is angry,
but she doesn't shout. At worst, she will grit her teeth and hold
her tears back, and it was that, 'We know who the killers are' [the
last line of the poem] said in a calm, strong, powerful way, that
I wanted to capture. It was my anger, mixed with the tenacity,

steadfastness and controlled anger of the Lawrence family that I was trying to blend together.

People sometimes describe my poetry as 'dub' poetry, but that is really just another word for reggae poetry. In the late 60s and early 70s, when Jamaicans started making reggae music, they made it in small cheap recording studios, where the musician would have to do it on one take. Then, because they wanted the record out quickly, they couldn't afford to record a 'B' side, so they would let the tape run again, and do an instrumental version, which was called a dub version, where the sound was dubbed in and dubbed out. Now it is called a 'remix' and a 'dance mix'. The DJ, who would be playing the Bob Marley song, or whatever, at a dance, would get asked by someone to play the dub. Then the DJ would flip the record over, play the dub, and they would employ someone like me to come and improvise over it.

The language I use in my poems is quite varied. There is a poem called 'A bomb pusher writes' in a book called *City Psalms*. That is not a poem I would perform, and in that poem, I am trying to imitate the voice of a well-educated, uniformed, military man with a very upper-class accent. He is an arms dealer and I am using someone else's voice. At other times, I find the English language restricting, and I want to play with it, and sound like two people cursing in the street, saying 'You tink I'm gonna believe *dat*?' And if I am going to capture that, I want to write it as phonetically true as possible. I used to sound much more Jamaican than I do now. But when I came down to London from Birmingham, and did my first press interviews, I was completely misunderstood, so I had to change a bit. But in my raw state, my poetry is very Jamaican.

One of my favourite poets is Miss Louise Bennett, the mother of all dub poets. Another of my favourites is Shelley! I love reading older English poems. I used to resist writing that stuff, but I have used some of those traditional forms in my last book of poems. *Too Black, Too Strong* is a very strong and a very black book in one sense, because of the issues, but I also have a pastiche of Larkin. I used to wonder if I should resist doing something like that because I am black, but I don't think like that now. I like writing in different styles.

My most popular poem, which has become a kind of national favourite, is 'Talking Turkeys', which is a *funny* poem. Whether I am at the opening of a museum in Handsworth, or at a militant vegan fair, everybody always asks me do that poem. It seems to have affected people from all classes and all races. The first line, 'Be nice to yu turkeys dis christmas' usually gets applause or laughter, because this poem gives the turkey a kind of character, which people identify with. At Christmas every year my agent phones me telling of all the requests for me to perform it. Some people have even stopped eating turkey for Christmas after hearing the poem, whereas if I hammer people over the head with heavy politics, it would turn them off. It is not really about conversion, but about making people think about it – so it, too, is a political poem.

Another poem which got unusual attention was 'What Stephen Lawrence Has Taught Us'. Channel 4 News broadcast it three times. Also when I wrote 'The Men from Jamaica Are Settling Down', which is about the ship SS *Empire Windrush*, which really began the great wave of post-war migration from the Caribbean to Britain, people were booking me to just perform that one, long, poem. Of course it is not as long as something like 'The Revolt of Islam' by Shelley, or something like that, but it is a long poem to perform on stage.

In a way, I wish that, for want of a better term, the white world, would pick up on those poems as much as they pick up on my animal poems and my funny poems. But it doesn't really bother me. 'Talking Turkeys' was voted something like the fifth favourite poem of all time by that BBC poll that Griff Rhys Jones used to do every National Poetry Day, and I can't see a poem like

'Knowing Me' or 'What Stephen Lawrence Has Taught Us' taking off in the same way. On the whole, people want to remember the good times. Even with music, political songs may move people, but they are not what people walk around singing and humming.

I don't like being described as a political activist. It almost makes me feel guilty, because I think I am not doing enough. Sometimes this surprises people, but I think that what I do is just being a citizen who wants to get involved in the society that I live in. I think that what I do, we should all do. I don't think it is anything special. You are white, and I don't think it is good enough for you to say, 'I'm not a racist.' You can genuinely think that you do not attack black people, you do not insult them, but, because you are not racist you feel that you can walk past the racist incident, feeling, 'Well! I'm not doing it.' The anti-racist says, 'I'm not standing for that.' You have to take a stand, even if it is through writing, or in whatever way you can.

My father was quite violent towards my mother, and there was a time when I was also violent towards my girlfriend. Then I had to stop and look at myself, and say, 'No, I've got to stop this violence.' And when I stopped hitting my girlfriend, I felt it was my duty to talk about it, because I know that some men do get in this cycle, and they need help. I thought, well, my dad did it, and all the people around me did, and if a man saw my woman doing something, he'd say, 'I saw your woman with another man. What you gonna do about it, man? Box her, man. Control your woman!' I thought, to be a man, I had to do that. But it was no good for me to stop hitting my woman, and allowing all my friends to keep doing it. I had to go to my friends and say, 'Hey, no! You can be a man without doing that.'

I didn't study politics. All the things I care about, and do, and write about, I do because of personal experience. I learnt my feminism from my mum, and I learnt my politics in the police station. I am proud of the honesty of my nakedness. I wrote a poem, and made a television programme, about being infertile and not being able to have kids. In a black community, black men don't talk about that. I was involved, on television with a poem called 'The Trouble With Men', and I went to Robert Winston and he tested me, and it actually exposed on television, the fact that I have got no sperm at all. Some people have a low sperm count, but I have a no sperm count. Thousands of black men wrote to me afterwards, and said, 'Wow! Good! Great! I've got that problem too.' But I was also attacked by other black men who said, 'You shouldn't talk about those things in front of white people.'

In the poem 'Childless' I am looking at myself. I am 47 – no one usually believes it, because I am so fit, perhaps because I am vegan, and I look younger than my age. I am a very fast sprinter, a very high jumper, a very high kicker. I run every day, I've got my own gymnasium, and yet that bit of me doesn't work! I can't believe it. So in the poem 'Childless' I am saying, 'Strong biceps / Firm thighs,' it's all working 'In there / Somewhere, / There must be / A baby / in here.' But again, many black men were shocked by this poem.

Black people were also shocked when I turned down the OBE! Most of them would say, 'Oh God, the Queen has invited me. I've got to do it.' But I said, 'No. I want to be true to myself and be able to look myself in the face in the morning.' I took a long time to reply, because I wanted to reject it in a 2,000-word article in the *Guardian*. That article has been translated into so many languages, many more than my poems or novels. First you get a letter from Tony Blair saying, in strict confidence, he is calling you before the Queen to join the Order of the British Empire, and you tick a box, yes, or no. To me, it sounds like joining the slavery club. Lots of people have turned it down, like David Bowie, but most people do it really quietly. But I felt there is so much frustration in the black community now about our art and history that has been robbed and is lying in British museums. We rightly commemorate the Holocaust, and make people realize that it should never happen again, but when it comes to talking about slavery, we have a chip on our shoulder.

There is a whole legacy of white supremacy that tells young black kids in school today that they will never be as good as the white man, so they don't want to do academic stuff, they want to be a rapper or a boxer. We talk about this all the time, but we say, 'White people are so proud of their Empire, don't say anything in front of them. Tell them they gave us cricket, and roads and the civil service.' I just thought, 'No'. There is no doubt that there are some good remnants of the Empire, but why couldn't we get that without all the rape and pillage? So there is the historical aspect, and also the modern-day one.

A couple of weeks before Tony Blair offered me the OBE, I was outside Downing Street, demonstrating about the death of my cousin in custody, wanting to hand a petition over to him, which he refused to come out and collect. It was all so frustrating. I was demonstrating against the war against Iraq, too, which I believed to be illegal, and he was writing me letters inviting me to come in because he was having a few poets round. He does this thing where he has poets and singers round to look cool. I had also written a poem, which opens *Too Black, Too Strong*, which makes it clear that I would never accept an award like that. I said in my statement, why didn't you offer me an award for my work in animal rights, or supporting people whose family died in custody, or fighting racism? Why was it a wishy-washy thing about literature? There are lots of better poets than me around.

Nowadays I don't have much faith in mainstream politics, so it is not a Labour or Tory or Liberal Democrat thing. I think a lot of politicians feel that they have to be seen to be being nice to black people, and lesbians, and gays. So they think, who can we give an OBE to, to make it look really inclusive? Oh, Benjamin Zephaniah! He's *very* well known. I mean, he's a bit radical, but he's 40-something now, and he's on the BBC all the time, Radio 4, he must have mellowed down, let's give it to him.'

I don't have any great ambitions. I just want to keep doing what I do, but I want to do it better, and reach more people. I love poetry, and I don't think I am going to run out of things to write about, because of the state of the world at the moment. I think poverty is going to be around for a long time, and the poor will still be exploited. Deep down, I really think I am a revolutionary. I do think you have got to find another way of doing things, but we can do that without violence. I don't want to be considered an award-winning poet. That doesn't say anything about my compassion or my love. I want people to say, 'Here is someone who is desperately trying to love everybody, and is trying to spread that love.'

My problem is that I am a workaholic. I think that I am here for a short time, and I have got to do as much as I can so that when I leave the world it is a little bit better than it was. I know that I have made a difference. Let me give you an example: a few years ago, I was performing in South Africa. An Asian man came up to me and said, 'When I was in exile in Dublin, I remember coming and listening to you perform in a little pub, and you said something that had a profound effect on me about creativity in education. I am now Minister of Education, and I have a programme of arts in education, which is directly inspired by the things you said.' And I thought 'Wow!'

I don't want to sound like I am blowing my own trumpet, even though this interview is about me, I suppose. But these are the things that keep me going. There are some times when I feel low and think, 'The *Daily Mail* have attacked me again. Do I really want to expose myself in public?' But every now and again it is all worthwhile. Some time ago a woman told me she was going to kill herself, and she turned the television up to throw herself over the balcony. And as she turned it up, I came on, doing a poem called 'Hurting World' about dying, and she felt as though

I had just come to talk to her personally at that time. I know I am not going to change the world, or start the revolution, but I can inspire people in small ways, and that is the best I can do. My poetry doesn't come from a great education, or a great knowledge of literature, it comes from experience, and from a passion for life, and a passion to better people's lives, and also a passion for music – the music of words.

I want to tell you one more story, if I may. I was performing in a school in Gloucester once. A kid asked me what I did as a hobby, and I said, 'Martial arts and kung fu.' He said, 'What kind?' and I replied, 'Wing Chun', and he said, pointing to a little boy in the front, 'Oh! He does Wing Chun.' So afterwards, I went up to the little boy, and we did a set of movements together, a bit like Tai Chi, but we have to touch each other to do them. It is a kind of soft sparring, an exercise almost like holding hands and folding hands over each other. We did it, and that was it.

About six months later, the teacher wrote to me and sent in a poem that the boy wrote to his father. His father was a member of Combat 18. One and eight are the first and eighth letter of the alphabet – AH – Adolph Hitler: they are like the military wing of the BNP. His father used to take him on rallies every weekend, and the boy wrote a poem saying, I met a black man and I liked him! The refrain of the poem was, 'Daddy, I don't want to be a racist no more.'

# Index